21ST CENTURY READING

CREATIVE THINKING AND READING WITH TEDTALKS

3

Laurie Blass • Mari Vargo • Ingrid Wisniewska

NATIONAL GEOGRAPHIC LEARNING | CENGAGE Learning

Australia • Brazil • Japan • Korea • Mexico • Singapore • Spain • United Kingdom • United States

21ˢᵗ Century Reading Student Book 3
Creative Thinking and Reading with
TED Talks

Laurie Blass

Mari Vargo

Ingrid Wisniewska

Publisher: Andrew Robinson

Executive Editor: Sean Bermingham

Associate Development Editor: Michelle Harris

Editorial Assistant: Dylan Mitchell

Director of Global Marketing: Ian Martin

Product Marketing Manager: Anders Bylund

Media Researcher: Leila Hishmeh

Director of Content and Media Production:
    Michael Burggren

Production Manager: Daisy Sosa

Senior Print Buyer: Mary Beth Hennebury

Cover and Interior Designers: Scott Baker
    and Aaron Opie

Cover Image: John McWhorter:
    ©James Duncan Davidson/TED

Composition: Cenveo® Publisher Services

For permission to use material from this text or product, submit all requests online at **cengage.com/permissions**

Further permissions questions can be emailed to **permissionrequest@cengage.com**

Student Book
ISBN 13: 978-1-305-26571-4

National Geographic Learning/Cengage Learning
20 Channel Center Street
Boston, MA 02210
USA

Cengage Learning is a leading provider of customised learning solutions with office locations around the globe, including Singapore, the United Kingdom, Australia, Mexico, Brazil and Japan. Locate our local office at **international.cengage.com/region**

Cengage Learning products are represented in Canada by Nelson Education Ltd.

Visit National Geographic Learning online at **NGL.Cengage.com**
Visit our corporate website at **www.cengage.com**

Printed in the United States of America
Print Number: 02   Print Year: 2015

SCOPE AND SEQUENCE

Unit/Theme	Lesson A Reading	Reading Skills	Critical Thinking
1 HIDDEN MIRACLES *Life Science*	*Viewing Nature's Beauty Through a New Lens* Interview	• Understanding reasons • Understanding key details • Paraphrasing ideas	• Interpreting a statement • Reflecting on own experience
2 SLEEP MATTERS *Health Science*	*Are You Sleeping Enough?* Scientific report	• Identifying reasons and effects • Understanding statistics • Understanding infographics	• Analyzing a writer's claims • Evaluating an argument
3 CYBORG TECH *Engineering / Technology*	*We Are Cyborgs* Expository article	• Understanding main ideas and key details	• Analyzing an argument for evidence • Evaluating possible problems
4 HAPPY PLANET *Economics / Statistics*	*The Road to Happiness?* Argumentative article	• Linking ideas using a summary chart • Analyzing an argument • Understanding infographics	• Evaluating an argument • Questioning statements in a text
5 CAREER PATHS *Business / Design*	*My Year in the Arctic* Personal blog	• Understanding sequence • Understanding reasons • Understanding figurative language	• Evaluating pros and cons • Interpreting a statement
6 TEXT GENERATION *Linguistics*	*The Death of Writing?* Explanatory article	• Understanding key details • Making comparisons • Understanding contrastive language	• Interpreting meaning
7 BARRIERS AND BRIDGES *Sociology*	*Bringing the World Together* Personal blog	• Understanding tone and purpose using a concept map	• Evaluating an argument using examples
8 PERSONALITY TYPES *Psychology*	*The Importance of Solitude* Personal recount / persuasive essay	• Understanding sequence • Identifying different viewpoints • Understanding classifications	• Making inferences • Evaluating an argument using examples
9 SMART THINKING *Behavior / Life Science*	*Nature of Intelligence* Scientific article	• Understanding key details • Inferring conclusions • Understanding reference	• Applying ideas to other contexts
10 FACING FEAR *Psychology / Exploration*	*Keep Calm!* Expository article	• Linking ideas and examples • Creating a map of the text • Understanding a process	• Questioning statements in a text • Applying ideas to other contexts

Lesson B	TED Talks	Academic Skills	Critical Thinking	Project
	Hidden Miracles of the Natural World Louie Schwartzberg	• Understanding main ideas and key details • Connecting ideas using a concept map • Making predictions	• Making predictions	• Researching for a presentation on biomimicry
	How to Succeed? Get More Sleep Arianna Huffington	• Understanding main ideas and classifications • Understanding metaphors • Understanding a speaker's message	• Evaluating an argument • Synthesizing ideas from multiple sources	• Researching for a presentation about sleep
	I Listen to Color Neil Harbisson	• Understanding key details • Understanding a process	• Reflecting on own viewpoint • Comparing similarities to other contexts	• Researching for a presentation on cyborg technology
	The Happy Planet Index Nic Marks	• Identifying key details • Recognizing a speaker's message • Recognizing main ideas and examples	• Questioning survey results • Applying information to own context	• Designing a plan for community happiness
	The Power of Time Off Stefan Sagmeister	• Understanding main ideas and key details • Making predictions • Understanding causes and effects	• Synthesizing information • Evaluating pros and cons • Applying ideas to own context	• Creating a time-off plan for employees
	Txtng is Killing Language. JK!!! John McWhorter	• Understanding key details • Making predictions • Applying information to new contexts • Summarizing information	• Evaluating an argument • Applying ideas to own experience	• Presenting an analysis of how people use texting
	The Danger of a Single Story Chimamanda Ngozi Adichie	• Understanding key details • Understanding a sequence of events • Understanding a process • Identifying main ideas	• Synthesizing ideas • Applying ideas to own context	• Critically evaluating an example of cultural stereotyping
	The Power of Introverts Susan Cain	• Understanding key details • Understanding cause and effect • Understanding a speaker's message	• Reflecting on own experience • Applying ideas to other contexts	• Researching for a presentation on contributions to society
	The Gentle Genius of Bonobos Susan Savage-Rumbaugh	• Understanding main ideas and key details • Understanding a speaker's message • Understanding sequence	• Reflecting on own experience	• Proposing and justifying a wildlife research project
	What I Learned from Going Blind in Space Chris Hadfield	• Recognizing and understanding main ideas • Interpreting descriptions • Understanding a sequence of events	• Interpreting meaning	• Designing a 3-day course for tackling phobias

WHAT IS 21ST CENTURY READING?

21ST CENTURY READING develops essential knowledge and skills for learners to succeed in today's global society. The series teaches core academic language skills and incorporates 21st century themes and skills such as global awareness, information literacy, and critical thinking.

Each unit of 21st Century Reading has three parts:

- **READ** about a 21st century topic—such as cyborg technology—in Lesson A.
- **LEARN** more about the topic by viewing an authentic TED Talk in Lesson B.
- **EXPLORE** the topic further by completing a collaborative research project.

VOCABULARY BUILDING

READING SKILLS

LANGUAGE SKILLS

Strategies for understanding key ideas, language use, and purpose.

BUSINESS AND TECHNOLOGY

GLOBAL AWARENESS

21ST CENTURY THEMES

Interdisciplinary topics that affect everyone in a global society.

LEARNING SKILLS

The "4 Cs" that all learners need for success in a complex world.

CRITICAL THINKING AND COMMUNICATION

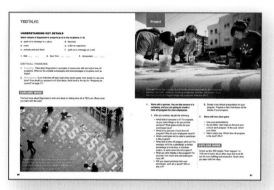

CREATIVITY AND COLLABORATION

21ST CENTURY LITERACIES

The ability to deal with information in a variety of modern formats and media.

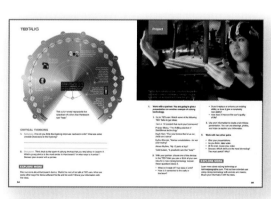

VISUAL LITERACY

INFORMATION AND MEDIA LITERACIES

➜ For more on 21st century learning, see **www.p21.org** and **21foundation.com**.

GOALS

IN THIS UNIT, YOU WILL:

- Read about a person who captures amazing images of nature.
- Learn about a new way of viewing the world.
- Explore how the natural world has inspired the development of new technology and inventions.

THINK AND DISCUSS

1. What are some things in nature that we cannot see with our own eyes?

2. Binoculars and microscopes are tools that help us look at nature more closely. Can you think of other examples? Which ones have you used?

HIDDEN
MIRACLES

A male hummingbird pollinating
an orchid

PRE-READING

A. Look at the photos on pages 10–13. What do you think each one shows? Read the captions to check your ideas.

B. Answer the following questions about the passage on pages 11–13.

1. Read the introduction. Who is the passage about? What is his profession?

   _____

   _____

2. What kinds of things do you think time-lapse photography can show us?

   _____

   _____

3. Read the sentences in bold in the passage. List the topics you think the passage will cover. Share your ideas with a partner.

   _____

   _____

   _____

   _____

   _____

4. Skim the entire passage. What kind of passage is this?

   a. An art book excerpt

   b. A science article

   c. An interview

Close-up of a caterpillar's mouth as seen under an electron microscope

Filmmaker Louie Schwartzberg has shot everything from TV commercials to documentaries, but he is best known for his time-lapse photography, a technique that captures images on film very slowly. When shown at regular speed, the viewer can see things the human eye cannot normally see. Schwartzberg's remarkable documentary—*Mysteries of the Unseen World*—**illustrates** his talent for capturing the wonders of nature using this technique.

VIEWING NATURE'S BEAUTY THROUGH A NEW LENS

National Geographic *spoke with Louie Schwartzberg about the* **challenges** *and rewards of his career in photography, the* **issues** *he feels most passionate about, and why he believes it's important that we all become more connected to nature.*

How did you become interested in nature photography and filmmaking?

1 I found my voice with photography as a student at UCLA [the University of California at Los Angeles]. We had anti-war protests going on right outside my classroom, so I picked up a camera and started to **document** that. And when I met my greatest teacher,

then I fell in love with nature. He taught me everything about lighting, composition, color, and how to live a sustainable, creative life.

Can you explain a little more about your Moving Art project and what the mission is?

2 Basically, I've got a thousand hours of material that I've filmed over the years. The mission is to be able to share how cool nature is—there's amazing time-lapse, slow motion, and aerials. You may have heard of nature deficit disorder,

---

aerials: *n.* images that are taken from above, as from an airplane

anti-war protests: *n.* demonstrations that express opposition to war

where kids are suffering from the fact that they're not connected to nature, but I think what we need to do is engage them where they are. That's what I'm trying to do.

You've been shooting time-lapse 24/7 for over three decades. What have you been shooting?

3 Flowers, **primarily**. They kind of seduce you with their beauty and you fall in love with them. That's why I made a film about pollination, which is so critical. A third of our food comes from pollinating plants. But to answer your question **specifically**, I've got two cameras going nonstop 24 hours a day, seven days a week, because time is precious and I don't want to waste a single second. I've squeezed 35 years of shooting into 12 hours of material.

What are some of the challenges that you deal with when you're time-lapse filmmaking?

4 The biggest ones, I think, are mosquitoes. They come out at sunset, at early dawn, and at twilight. . . . but besides the mosquitoes, when I'm on location, it's about survival. I've got to figure out food, water, transportation, and how to get back home when it gets dark. It's not just the technique, but I do it because I think time-lapse can **transform** your consciousness by helping you see things from a different point of view. That's when you change your perspective. And when you change your perspective, that's how you develop gratitude.

What's one of the most memorable experiences you've had in nature while doing your work?

5 I was recently in Panama shooting hummingbirds in slow motion. It's just amazing to see their world. They're very territorial with the way they kind of fight each other to get the flower. And nectar-feeding bats in the Sonoran Desert—I got this incredible shot of a baby bat breastfeeding on the mother bat as the mom is feeding on a flower in the desert. Most people don't realize the entire Sonoran Desert would not exist without these nectar-feeding bats.

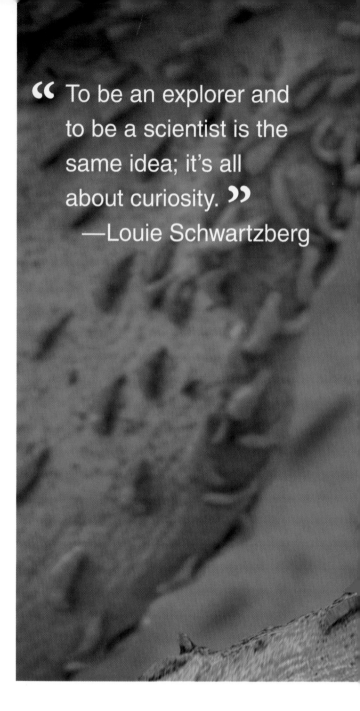

❝ To be an explorer and to be a scientist is the same idea; it's all about curiosity. **❞**
—Louie Schwartzberg

What environmental issues mean the most to you right now?

6 I think [bee] colony collapse disorder would be at the top. I've heard scientists say it could be way more serious than climate change. And there's a quote **attributed to** Einstein that if the bees ever disappeared, man would only have four years left to live. It doesn't really matter whether it's true or whether Einstein said it or not. The healthiest food we need to eat—fruits, nuts, seeds, and vegetables—would disappear without pollinating plants. It's pretty serious.

A butterfly's egg magnified under an electron microscope

What would you say is one of the most surprising things you've learned in your career?

7 I keep getting the same things **reinforced** over and over. When I film things, I'm connecting with the universal rhythms of the universe, which is the deepest part of my soul. And it's this **constant** reminder that it's all connected. I also think we always have to be curious, and nature really inspires you to be an explorer [. . .]. To be an explorer and to be a scientist is the same idea; it's all about curiosity. And I think the same thing is true being a filmmaker or an artist. We have different rules, but we're both trying to share the wonders of nature and the universe with people.

[bee] colony collapse disorder: *n.* a mysterious condition that is killing bees and weakening their colonies

gratitude: *n.* thankfulness, appreciation

pollination: *n.* the action of transferring pollen to the stigma of a plant so that it can reproduce

shooting: *v.* taking photographs (of)

twilight: *n.* the period between sunset and darkness

GETTING THE MAIN IDEAS

What main points does Schwartzberg make in this interview? Check (✓) three ideas he mentions.

1. _____ It's important for young people to feel more engaged with nature.

2. _____ More investment is needed to improve time-lapse filmmaking technology.

3. _____ Time-lapse can help people see the world from a different perspective.

4. _____ People should always be curious about the world around them.

5. _____ Photography is important for anti-war movements around the world.

6. _____ Time-lapse has helped make people more aware of climate change.

▲ A close-up image of a flea seen under an electron microscope

UNDERSTANDING REASONS

Expressions such as *that's why, because*, and *so* can help a reader understand the connections between ideas and the reasons for them. However, sometimes the reasons behind an idea are implied and not clearly stated; they are not connected to ideas with specific words or phrases.

Match the reasons (a–f) with the ideas below. Use the information in the passage to help you. Two reasons are extra.

a. He was able to get a unique photograph of a baby bat in mid-flight.

b. A lot of our most important food would disappear if there were no bees.

c. Pollinating plants are beautiful, and they are important for our survival.

d. There's so little time and so many things to capture on film.

e. He wants to use time-lapse photography to change people's perspective.

f. Some protests were going on outside his classroom at UCLA.

Idea	Reason
Schwartzberg specializes in photographing flowers.	
Schwartzberg has cameras going continuously, 24 hours a day, seven days a week.	
Schwartzberg is willing to deal with many challenges to capture his images.	
Schwartzberg believes colony collapse is the most important environmental issue.	

B. Choose the correct definition for each of the bold words.

1. The quotation "Look deep into nature, and then you will understand everything better" is **attributed to** Albert Einstein.

   a. believed to be from

   b. a way to describe

2. Climate change is one of the most important environmental **issues** that we face today.

   a. topics

   b. documents

3. Extreme weather events present a **constant** reminder that global warming is a serious problem.

   a. conflicting

   b. continuous

4. You can **reinforce** an appreciation of nature by taking city children on wilderness field trips.

   a. strengthen

   b. introduce

5. Spending a few days in the wilderness can completely **transform** the way some children see the world.

   a. confuse

   b. change

6. Some photographers travel the world **documenting** the lives of people in war-torn countries.

   a. providing evidence for

   b. making a record of

GETTING MEANING FROM CONTEXT

Note answers to the questions and discuss your ideas with a partner.

1. What do you think Louie Schwartzberg means when he says, "I found my voice with photography"?

   _____

2. What does Schwartzberg mean by a "nature deficit disorder"?

   _____

CRITICAL THINKING

1. Interpreting. Look again at Schwartzberg's answer to the final question in the interview. How does he compare explorers and scientists with filmmakers and artists? What do you think he means by "different rules"? Explain your ideas to a partner.

2. Reflecting. Have you seen any images—in photographs or on film—that have changed your thinking or the way that you view the world? If so, describe the images and explain how they changed your perspective.

EXPLORE MORE

See more of Louie Schwartzberg's images of the natural world by watching his TED Talk "The hidden beauty of pollination." What does it reveal about the relationship between plants and insects? Share your information with the class.

HIDDEN MIRACLES OF THE NATURAL WORLD

LOUIE SCHWARTZBERG Filmmaker, TED speaker

⌂ Like many of us, Louie Schwartzberg has always loved looking at beautiful flowers. In doing so, he has realized something important about them: They help us understand that everything is connected in the natural world.

After graduating from college, Schwartzberg decided to live a simple life in the countryside. He had no phone and no TV. With few distractions, he had all the time in the world to follow his passion: filming flowers using time-lapse photography. His work has helped him understand the connections between different plants and animals—including humans. He believes that our connection to nature can bring great happiness. He believes it can help us live in the moment and be grateful for what we have.

Today, Schwartzberg hopes that his work will not only help people find happiness in the beauty of nature, but also inspire them to protect and sustain the planet.

---

sustain: *v.* to keep in existence by providing support, strength, or necessities

Schwartzberg's **idea worth spreading** is that technology enables us to see things differently. It can change our beliefs about nature and our place in it.

In this lesson, you are going to watch Schwartzberg's talk. Use the information on page 18 to answer each question.

1. How do you think Schwartzberg's lifestyle choices after college contributed to his later work?

   _____

2. What two effects does Schwartzberg hope his work will have?

   _____

PART 1

A NEW WAY OF SEEING

PREVIEWING

A. Read the excerpt below from Schwartzberg's talk. What do you think you will see in *Mysteries of the Unseen World*?

_____

_____

B. What words do you think are missing in the excerpt? Check your ideas as you watch (▶) the first segment of the TED Talk.

❝ What is the intersection between technology, art, and science? Curiosity and wonder, because it drives us to explore, because we're _____ by things we can't see. And
                                                                                            1

I love to use film to take us on a _____ through portals of time and space, to
                                                             2

make the invisible visible, because what that does, it _____ our horizons, it
                                                                                       3

transforms our perception, it _____ our minds, and it touches our heart. So here
                                                         4

are some scenes from my 3D IMAX film, *Mysteries of the Unseen World*. ❭❭

_____

intersection: *n.* a point where two or more things or ideas connect

portals: *n.* entrances, doors

UNDERSTANDING MAIN IDEAS

Check (✓) the two main ideas of this part of the talk.

Time-lapse can show us things that . . .

1. _____ are very old.

2. _____ move or grow very slowly.

3. _____ act in an unusual way.

4. _____ are extremely fast.

5. _____ occur very rarely.

▲ A brown-spotted yellow-wing dragonfly alights on a twig.

CONNECTING MAIN IDEAS AND DETAILS

A. Complete the mind map. Match the main ideas from Schwartzberg's talk with the examples.

a. air flow

b. insect movement

c. hovering

d. ships at sea

e. clouds

f. flying backwards

g. four wings in different directions

h. air traffic data

i. aurora borealis

j. lightning

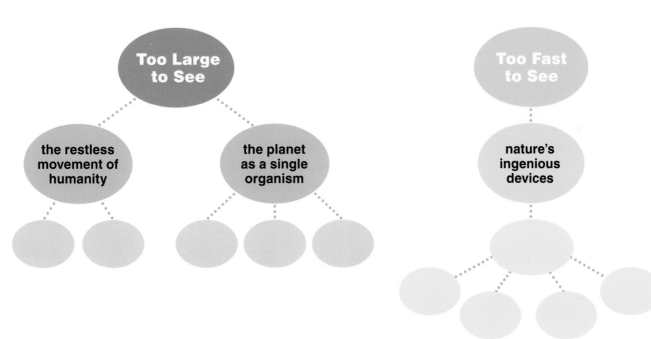

B. Now use the mind map and information from this part of the talk to answer these questions.

1. Why does Schwartzberg say the dragonfly is the greatest flier in nature?

_____

2. According to Schwartzberg, what kinds of devices might we be able to create as a result of seeing insect movement close up?

_____

CRITICAL THINKING

Predicting. What else do you think time-lapse photography might allow us to see? Would it be mainly to capture the beauty of nature, or do you think there could be some practical application?

PART 2

STRANGE NEW WORLDS

PREDICTING

What do you think these images show? Work with a partner to match each picture with a caption. Check your ideas as you watch (▶) the next part of Schwartzberg's talk.

a. a snail's tongue   **b.** a fruit fly's eye   **c.** shark skin   **d.** an eggshell

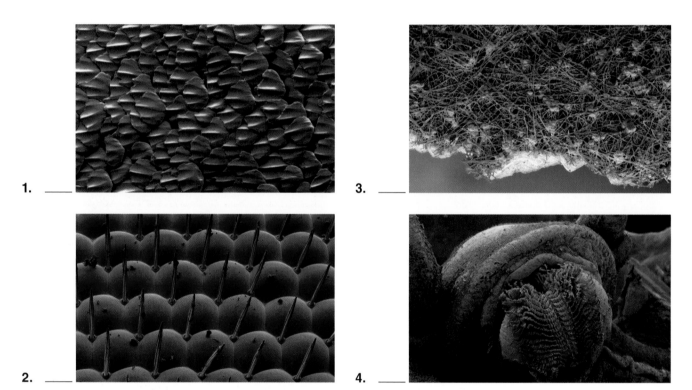

1. ____

2. ____

3. ____

4. ____

UNDERSTANDING KEY DETAILS

Use information from Schwartzberg's TED Talk to answer these questions.

1. What is special about spider silk?

   It is _____ than human hair but _____ than steel.

2. What might nano devices be able to do someday?

   Patrol our bodies for _____, _____ arteries, and _____ DNA.

EXPLORE MORE

Find out more about Louie Schwartzberg's film *Mysteries of the Unseen World* at movies.nationalgeographic.com. Share your information with the class.

Project

An Olympic swimmer wearing a swimsuit made of fabric based on shark skin

A. **Work with a partner. You are going to find out about how something in nature has inspired a particular technology or invention.**

1. Go to TED.com. Watch some of the following TED Talks to get ideas for nature-inspired inventions:

   • Janine Benyus, "Biomimicry in action"
   • Hamish Jolly, "A shark-deterrent wetsuit"
   • Michael Pawlyn, "Using nature's genius in architecture"
   • Cheryl Hayashi, "The magnificence of spider silk"
   • Markus Fischer, "A robot that flies like a bird"

2. With your partner, choose one of the technologies or inventions in the TED Talks you saw, and answer these questions about it.

   • What is the invention or technology?
   • What thing (animal, plant, etc.) in nature inspired the invention? Describe the properties that seem particularly useful or interesting.
   • How does the invention or technology work?
   • What are its applications?

3. Use your information to create a two-minute presentation. You can use drawings, photos, and video to explain your information.

B. **Work with two other pairs.**

   • Give your presentations.
   • As you listen, take notes.
   • At the end, review your notes.
   • Discuss: Which invention inspired by nature is the most interesting to you? Why?

EXPLORE MORE

Learn more about how nature has inspired new inventions and technologies at ngm.nationalgeographic. com/geopedia/Biomimetics. Share your information with the class.

SLEEP MATTERS

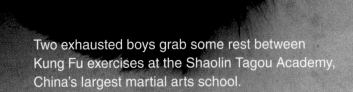

Two exhausted boys grab some rest between Kung Fu exercises at the Shaolin Tagou Academy, China's largest martial arts school.

PRE-READING

A. Note answers to the questions below, and share your ideas with a partner.

1. What factors do you think help you get a good night's sleep?

_____

_____

2. How many hours of sleep do you think people your age typically get each night?

_____

3. Look at the infographic on page 28. According to the information given, how much sleep should you get every night? Do you get this much sleep? If not, why not?

_____

_____

B. Look at the two headings in the reading. Predict the information that each section might contain.

1. Why do many people feel they don't have enough time to sleep?

_____

_____

2. What are some effects of lack of sleep, or "sleep deprivation"?

_____

_____

A tired student takes a nap on a classroom desk during lunch break. Lack of sleep is a common problem among young adults.

ARE YOU SLEEPING ENOUGH?

1 We've all had restless nights when we couldn't get to sleep—and have suffered the next day as a result. Sleep experts say the average adult requires seven to nine hours of sleep per night; in fact, anything less could harm our health.

NO TIME TO SLEEP

2 In spite of the importance of sleep, many people are not getting enough. For example, Americans sleep one hour less per night on average than they did 20 to 30 years ago. "The dependency on caffeine and the whole Starbucks culture is certainly one proof that our society is sleepier than ever before," says William Dement, a sleep researcher at Stanford University. Sleep is a biological need, much like food and water. If totally deprived of shut-eye, humans **ultimately** perish. Yet millions of people are increasingly skimping on their sleep.

3 Why has sleep deprivation become such a big problem? There are a couple of possible reasons. Researchers say that today's sleep deprivation is partly due to modern expectations. These days, consumers expect information, entertainment, and food to be available round-the-clock. One of the results of this 24/7 culture is that consumers stay awake longer and later than they used to. Consequently, workers who provide us with goods and services can't stop working when the sun goes down. In addition, the fast-paced and competitive world of business often rewards employees for arriving at work early and staying late. As a result, many employees are willing to skip sleep in order to impress the boss.

EFFECTS OF SLEEP DEPRIVATION

4 Sleep deprivation can have a significantly detrimental impact on our performance, however. According to Charles Czeisler of Harvard University, staying awake for 24 hours or sleeping only five hours a night for a week is like having a blood-alcohol level of 0.1 percent. That is well above the **legal** limit for safe driving in most countries. Most people probably wouldn't get drunk before going to work or taking an exam; but if they are sleeping an average of five hours a night, they may be working, studying, driving, and making decisions as though they are intoxicated.

5 Sleep deprivation can result in poor grades or poor performance at work. But in some cases, it can have more dangerous effects. In February 2009, a commuter plane crashed on the way from Newark, New Jersey, to Buffalo, New York, killing all 49 people on board and one person on the ground. An **investigation** determined that the crash was most likely a result of fatigue. The copilot, and probably the pilot, had slept very little the day before the crash. Not surprisingly, sleep deprivation is linked to car accidents, too. The U.S. **Institute** of Medicine reports that almost 20 percent of car accidents happen because drivers are sleepy.

6 Sleep deprivation can be a particularly grave problem in the **medical** profession. In 2007, Czeisler researched the habits of 2,700 first-year medical residents. Most of these residents worked for extremely long periods, some working 30-hour-long shifts twice a

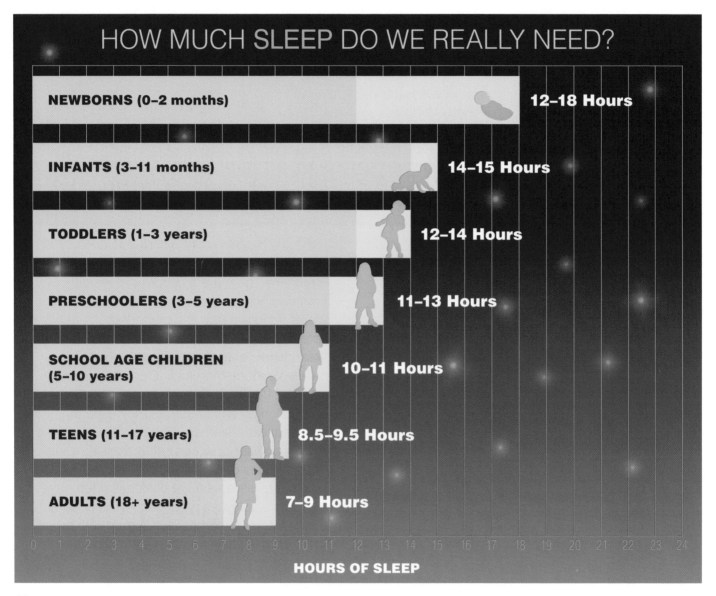

HOW MUCH SLEEP DO WE REALLY NEED?

NEWBORNS (0–2 months) 12–18 Hours

INFANTS (3–11 months) 14–15 Hours

TODDLERS (1–3 years) 12–14 Hours

PRESCHOOLERS (3–5 years) 11–13 Hours

SCHOOL AGE CHILDREN (5–10 years) 10–11 Hours

TEENS (11–17 years) 8.5–9.5 Hours

ADULTS (18+ years) 7–9 Hours

0 1 2 3 4 5 6 7 8 9 10 11 12 13 14 15 16 17 18 19 20 21 22 23 24

HOURS OF SLEEP

A man taking a nap on a train car in Cairo, Egypt. According to sleep researcher Carl Hunt, "Sleep is just as important for our overall health as are exercise and a healthy diet."

week. Many admitted that fatigue had had severe **consequences** on their performance and treatment of patients. Twenty percent of residents **acknowledged** making fatigue-related mistakes that led to **injury** of a patient. Five percent confessed that lack of sleep caused them to make a mistake that resulted in a patient's death.

7 We all know that we need sleep, but sleep deprivation continues to be a widespread problem around the world. Studies show that one in five adults suffer from daytime sleepiness. Among those aged 18 to 34, 50 percent say that daytime sleepiness interferes with their daily work. To many, the ability to function without much sleep is something to brag about. However, sleep is **crucial** to our well-being and our performance. It may be time to wake up and change our perspective on sleep.

---

brag: *v.* to talk about your achievements in a boastful or proud way

detrimental impact: *adj.* damaging or harmful effect

exhaustion: *n.* a state of extreme physical and/or mental tiredness

grave: *adj.* very serious

medical residents: *n.* medical school graduates undergoing on-the-job training

DEADLY DEPRIVATION

A complete lack of sleep can be deadly. In a sleep study performed by the prominent sleep researcher Allan Rechtschaffen at the University of Chicago, rats were kept awake and not permitted to sleep at all. After about two weeks, all of the rats died. The rats' organs were not damaged, and the rats didn't seem to have anything seriously wrong with them. **Apparently**, they all died from exhaustion.

GETTING THE MAIN IDEAS

Read the first sentence of a summary of the reading passage. Complete the summary by choosing the two sentences from the list that state the most important ideas in the passage.

Even though sleep is very important, many people these days are not getting enough.

_____ Some animals sleep up to 18 hours a day.

_____ Modern 24/7 culture is causing more people to suffer from a lack of sleep.

_____ In February of 2009, a commuter plane crashed on its way from Newark, New Jersey, to Buffalo, New York.

_____ Studies show that sleeping for at least eight hours after studying helps students remember what they've learned.

_____ Researchers are learning how sleep deprivation can have a significantly negative effect on performance.

_____ Exercising on a regular basis can help people sleep better, but exercising right before bedtime can make it difficult to fall asleep.

IDENTIFYING REASONS AND EFFECTS

It can be useful to create a summary map of a text, especially to help you understand relationships such as processes, sequences, and reasons and effects. These kinds of relationships frequently occur in scientific articles.

What are some of the reasons for and effects of sleep deprivation? Complete the summary with information from the reading.

Reasons for sleep deprivation
24/7 expectations
Culture people want _____ 1 , _____ 2 , _____ 3 24 hours a day
Business employees rewarded for _____ 4

Effects of sleep deprivation
Poor performance
School lower _____ 5
Work _____ 6 and drivers cause more fatigue-related _____ 7 ; medical residents make more _____ 8

UNDERSTANDING STATISTICS

A. **Find statistics in the passage to answer each question.**

According to the reading, what percentage of . . .

1. adults feel sleepy during the day? _____

2. younger adults feel that sleep deprivation affects their work? _____

3. medical residents say that sleepiness led to the death of a patient? _____

4. car accidents occurred because of tired drivers? _____

B. **Which of the statistics above do you think are similar in your own country? Which statistic do you find most surprising? Why? Note your ideas and discuss with a partner.**

_____

_____

UNDERSTANDING INFOGRAPHICS

A. **Complete the sentences based on the information in the infographic on page 28.**

1. _____ and _____ need more sleep than toddlers.

2. _____ need to sleep the fewest hours.

3. Teenagers need from _____ to _____ hours of sleep.

4. Four-year-old children need from _____ to _____ hours of sleep.

5. Toddlers need, on average, an hour more sleep than _____.

B. **Discuss these questions with a partner.**

1. Look at the information for adults' sleep needs. How do you think sleep requirements might vary within this category? For example, do older people need more or less sleep than people in their 30s? Explain.

2. What other information might be useful to include in this infographic? How else could the information be organized?

BUILDING VOCABULARY

A. Use these words from the passage to complete the paragraph below.

acknowledge   consequences   crucial   injure   medical

According to sleep experts, sleep is _____ for our health and
                                    1

performance. When we don't get enough sleep, we are more likely to get sick and make

mistakes. Sleep is especially important for people who work in the _____
        2

field. Doctors and nurses often work long hours. When they are sleepy, they might

accidentally _____ a patient or even cause a patient's death. Even
    3

though most people know that sleep is important, they continue to deprive themselves of

it. This is why it's important to _____ that lack of sleep is a significant
    4

problem. The _____ of sleep deprivation are just too serious to ignore.
    5

B. Circle the words that are closest in meaning to the words in bold. Some items
have more than one answer.

1. **institute**

   a. team   **b.** class   **c.** organization   **d.** classroom

2. **investigation**

   a. research   **b.** examination   **c.** lawsuit   **d.** problem

3. **legal**

   a. criminal   **b.** difficult   **c.** lawful   **d.** allowed

4. **ultimately**

   a. finally   **b.** quickly   **c.** eventually   **d.** realistically

5. **apparently**

   a. factually   **b.** seemingly   **c.** certainly   **d.** enthusiastically

C. Have there been any *investigations* reported in the news recently? Share your
ideas with a partner.

GETTING MEANING FROM CONTEXT

A. **Find these words and phrases (1–7) in the reading on pages 26–29. Match each one with the best definition (a–g).**

_____ **1.** totally deprived of shut-eye (paragraph 2)

a. suffering from complete lack of sleep

_____ **2.** skimping (paragraph 2)

b. understand something in a different way

_____ **3.** round-the-clock (paragraph 3)

c. not doing or getting as much as you should

_____ **4.** intoxicated (paragraph 4)

d. very probably

_____ **5.** most likely (paragraph 5)

e. all day; 24 hours a day

_____ **6.** fatigue (paragraph 5)

f. affected by alcohol or drugs; drunk

_____ **7.** change our perspective (paragraph 7)

g. a feeling of tiredness

B. **Can you think of a time when you "changed your perspective" on something? What caused it to change? Share your answer with a partner.**

_____

_____

CRITICAL THINKING

1. Analyzing. Use the chart to analyze three of the writer's claims. Are the writer's claims supported with quotes, statistics, or information from or about experts?

Claim	Quote?	Stat?	Expert?
Americans are sleeping less than they used to.			
Sleep deprivation is partly due to a 24/7 culture.			
Sleep deprivation can be deadly.			

2. Evaluating. What else could be included to make the writer's claims more convincing? Do you think the writer's overall argument is convincing? Why or why not?

EXPLORE MORE

Read more about why we need sleep at ngm.nationalgeographic.com/2010/05/sleep/max-text. Share what you learn with the class.

A boy yawns as he waits for customers at his ▶ roadside apple stall in Kabul, Afghanistan.

TEDTALKS

HOW TO SUCCEED? GET MORE SLEEP

ARIANNA HUFFINGTON Journalist, TED speaker

🎧 The lifestyle of a globetrotting media executive doesn't lend itself to getting deep, regular sleep. Arianna Huffington knows about this firsthand.

Huffington is the cofounder and editor-in-chief of *The Huffington Post*, one of the most popular news and blog sites on the Internet. She is also a journalist, the author of several books, and the host of popular political radio shows.

Born in Athens, Greece, Huffington moved to the United Kingdom at the age of 16. She attended the University of Cambridge, where she studied economics. She is now considered by many to be one of the most influential women in media. In 2014, she was included in *Forbes* magazine's list of "The World's 100 Most Powerful Women."

Huffington's career has brought her money and power, the two traditional "metrics of success," but recent experiences with sleep deprivation and exhaustion have caused Huffington to consider a possible third indicator of success. In her book *Thrive: The Third Metric to Redefining Success and Creating a Life of Well-Being, Wisdom, and Wonder*, Huffington explores the idea that true success requires mental, physical, and emotional health and well-being.

---

influential: *adj.* having the power to affect or control something or someone

lend itself: *idiom* to be suitable for (a particular purpose)

Arianna Huffington's **idea worth spreading** is that a good night's rest is a simple but powerful way to increase our productivity and happiness.

In this lesson, you are going to watch Arianna Huffington's TED Talk. Use the information on page 34 to answer each question.

1. Where was Huffington born, and where did she go to college?

   _____

2. What field of work is Huffington in now?

   _____

3. What is the main message of Huffington's book *Thrive*?

   _____

4. Why do you think she is regarded as one of the world's "most powerful women"?

   _____

PART 1

A JOURNEY OF REDISCOVERY

PREVIEWING

A. **Read these excerpts from Huffington's talk. Then discuss your answers to the questions below with a partner.**

❝ My big idea is a very, very small idea that can unlock billions of big ideas that are at the moment dormant inside us. And my little idea that will do that is sleep. ❞

❝ Two and a half years ago, I fainted from exhaustion. I hit my head on my desk. I broke my cheekbone, I got five stitches on my right eye. ❞

dormant: *adj.* hidden, unexpressed, undeveloped

1. Why do you think Huffington says her idea will unlock billions of big ideas? Whose ideas is she referring to?

2. Why do you think Huffington tells the story about fainting?

B. **Watch (▶) the first segment of Huffington's TED Talk to check your ideas.**

UNDERSTANDING MAIN IDEAS

A. **Read the excerpt from Huffington's talk. Choose the sentence that best paraphrases the excerpt.**

❝ I began the journey of rediscovering the value of sleep. And in the course of that, I studied, I met with medical doctors, scientists, and I'm here to tell you that the way to a more productive, more inspired, more joyful life is getting enough sleep. ❞

a. I did a lot of research on sleep and discovered that many medical doctors and scientists suffer from a serious lack of sleep.

b. I participated in sleep experiments with doctors and scientists, and I discovered that I had problems sleeping.

c. I studied a lot about the importance of sleep, and I discovered that getting enough sleep can lead to a better life.

B. **Write an answer to the question below.**

According to Huffington, what are some benefits of getting enough sleep?

_____

_____

UNDERSTANDING A CLASSIFICATION

Arianna Huffington refers to Type A people in her talk. Read the description of personality types, and discuss answers to the questions with a partner.

The Type A/Type B personality theory was developed by cardiologists Meyer Friedman and Ray Rosenman in the 1950s. The two doctors developed the theory after observing patients with heart conditions in the waiting room of their office. They noticed that some of the heart patients were unable to sit still, and these patients wore out the seats of the chairs by moving around nervously. Friedman and Rosenman labeled these people Type A and determined that a Type A person is more likely than another person to have heart disease and high blood pressure.

According to the theory, Type A people tend to be very competitive and rushed and they become angry more easily than other people. These individuals often have high-stress jobs and spend a lot of time working and striving to succeed. Type B individuals tend to be more relaxed, less anxious, and more creative and imaginative. There is also a Type C personality. These individuals tend to hold their emotions in, particularly negative ones like anger and frustration. They also avoid conflict and try to be nice to everyone.

Friedman and Rosenman's theory is not perfect—not everyone falls into one of these categories. However, people often use the term "Type A" to describe high-achieving, competitive individuals who lead stressful lives.

1. Which type of person do you think is the most likely to sleep well?

2. Which type do you think you are? Explain.

3. Think of people you know who fit into these three categories. Describe them.

4. Huffington says that most of her audience are "Type A" people. Why does she think they are especially sleep-deprived?

PART 2

A NEW REVOLUTION

UNDERSTANDING METAPHORS

A. **Huffington uses a metaphor (comparison) to make a point about leadership. Read the excerpt and complete the sentence to explain what she means.**

    ❝ . . . the essence of leadership is being able to see the iceberg before it hits the *Titanic*. And we've had far too many icebergs hitting our *Titanics*. ❞

What Huffington means is that a good leader should be able to _____.

    a. see a problem before it happens   **b.** come up with creative solutions after a problem occurs

B. **Watch (▶) the next segment of Huffington's TED Talk to check your ideas.**

UNDERSTANDING A SPEAKER'S MESSAGE

A. **Huffington believes that men and women value sleep differently. Answer the questions and share your ideas with a partner.**

1. Huffington says, "Sleep deprivation has become a virility symbol." What does she mean by *a virility symbol*? How might sleep deprivation be a virility symbol for some men?

A virility symbol is _____.

Some men try to express their virility by saying _____

_____.

2. Huffington tells a story about a dinner date with a man who bragged about getting only four hours of sleep the night before. Why do you think she tells this story?

_____

_____

B. **In the excerpt below, Huffington refers to Lehman Brothers (a large American financial services company that declared bankruptcy in 2008). What point is she making?**

❝ In fact, I have a feeling that if Lehman Brothers was Lehman Brothers and Sisters, they might still be around. While all the brothers were busy just being hyper-connected 24/7, maybe a sister would have noticed the iceberg, because she would have woken up from a seven-and-a-half or eight-hour sleep and have been able to see the big picture. ❞

_____

_____

CRITICAL THINKING

1. Evaluating. Do you agree or disagree with the way Huffington characterizes men and women in regards to sleep? Why or why not?

2. Synthesizing. How does Arianna Huffington's TED Talk support the main ideas of the reading passage on pages 26–29?

EXPLORE MORE

Learn about how our internal body clock can regulate our sleep schedule by watching Jessa Gamble's TED Talk "Our natural sleep cycle" on TED.com. Share what you learn with the class.

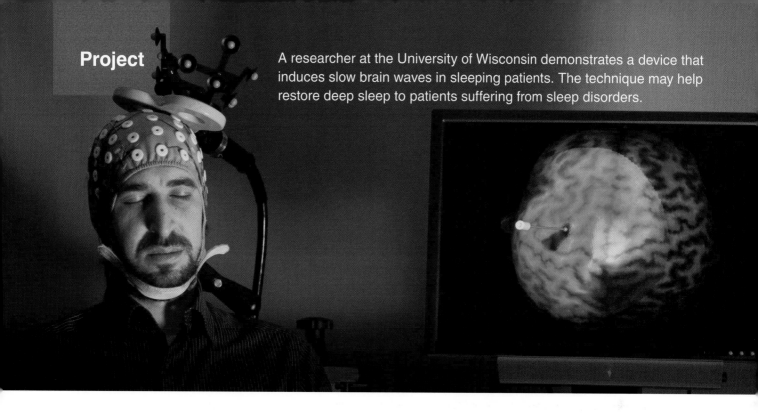

Project

A researcher at the University of Wisconsin demonstrates a device that induces slow brain waves in sleeping patients. The technique may help restore deep sleep to patients suffering from sleep disorders.

A. **Work with a partner. You are going to find out more about one of the sleep-related topics below.**

- The effects of modern technology (e.g., tablets, smartphones, television, computers) on sleep
- Ways to improve sleep
- Sleepwalking

- Other sleep disorders
- Why we dream
- (Your own idea): _____

_____

1. With your partner, choose the topic that you find the most interesting or come up with your own sleep-related topic.

2. Go online to learn as much as you can about the topic. Take notes on the most important and interesting information.

3. Use your information to create a two-minute presentation. You can use drawings, photos, and video to explain your information. Where possible, include real-life examples, case studies, and anecdotes to illustrate your ideas.

B. **Work with two other pairs.**

- Give your presentation to the other pairs.
- As you listen to the other pairs' presentations, take note of the key points. Review the information at the end of the presentations.

C. **Discuss these questions with your class.**

1. What new information did you learn? What was most surprising?

2. What topic do you want to learn more about?

EXPLORE MORE

Learn more about sleep by watching Russell Foster's TED Talk "Why do we sleep?" at TED.com. How does Foster describe the purpose of sleep? Share your information with the class.

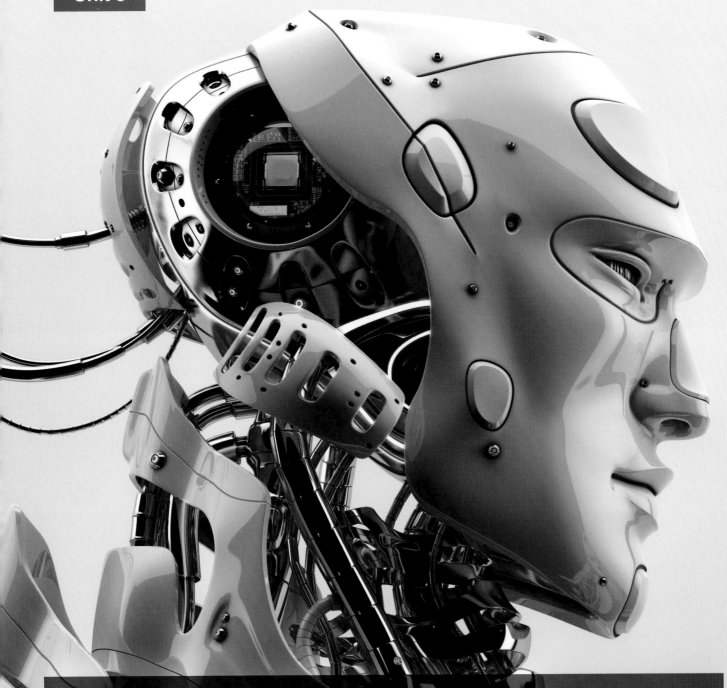

GOALS

IN THIS UNIT, YOU WILL:

- Read about technologies that enhance human abilities.
- Learn about a technology that lets a person hear colors.
- Explore other devices that replace or improve human abilities.

THINK AND DISCUSS

1. What are some devices that help people see and hear better?

2. In what ways might technology help us experience the world in the future?

CYBORG
TECH

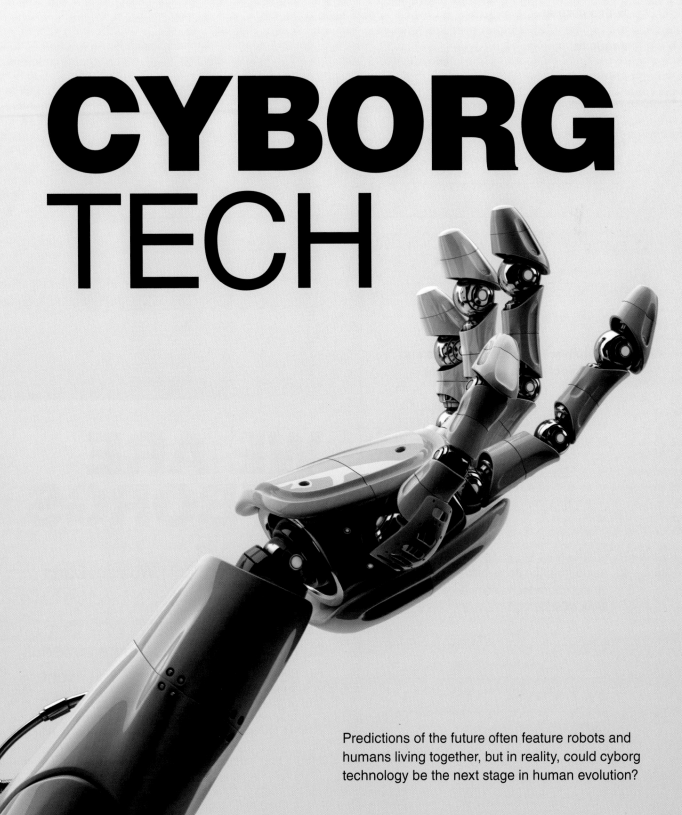

Predictions of the future often feature robots and humans living together, but in reality, could cyborg technology be the next stage in human evolution?

PRE-READING

A. **Look at the photos on pages 42–45 and read the captions. What do you think each device does? Discuss your ideas with a partner.**

Argus II:

_____

_____

Cochlear implant:

_____

_____

EyeTap:

_____

_____

B. **Note answers to these questions and discuss your ideas with a partner.**

1. Read the first paragraph on page 42. What is a cyborg? What are some examples of cyborgs?

_____

_____

_____

2. Aside from the items pictured, what other cyborg technology do you think exists?

_____

_____

Larry Hester testing out Argus II. The device includes a small video camera, a computer, a receiver, and an array of electrodes implanted on the patient's retina.

WE ARE CYBORGS

1 RoboCop, the Bionic Woman, Darth Vader—what do these characters have in common? They are all cyborgs—humans who are made more powerful by **advanced** technology. You might think that cyborgs exist only in fiction, or are a possibility only in the distant future. But cyborg technology already exists.

DEFINING CYBORGS

2 The word *cyborg*—a short form of "cybernetic organism"—was first used in a 1960 paper on space travel. A cyborg was defined as an organism "to which [external] **components** have been added for the purpose of **adapting** to new . . . environments." According to this definition, an astronaut in a spacesuit is an example of a cyborg, as the spacesuit helps the astronaut adapt to a new environment— space. More recently, the word has evolved to refer to human beings who have **mechanical** body parts that make them more than human.

REAL-LIFE CYBORGS

3 Although super-humans like RoboCop are not yet a reality, advances in real-life cyborg technology allow some people to compensate for abilities they have lost, and give other people new and unusual abilities. An example is filmmaker Rob Spence and his bionic eye. Spence injured one of his eyes in an accident. Instead of replacing his damaged eye with the typical glass eye, Spence had a prosthetic eye with a camera **implanted** in his eye socket. The eye is not connected to Spence's brain or optic nerve, but it can record what Spence sees. Spence has used his camera eye to record interviews for a documentary about people with bionic body parts.

---

bionic: *adj.* using mechanical and/or electrical devices to increase a person's ability

cybernetic: *adj.* relating to the connections between biological, mechanical, and electronic systems

optic nerve: *n.* a nerve that sends visual information from the retina to the brain

prosthetic: *adj.* relating to an artificial body part

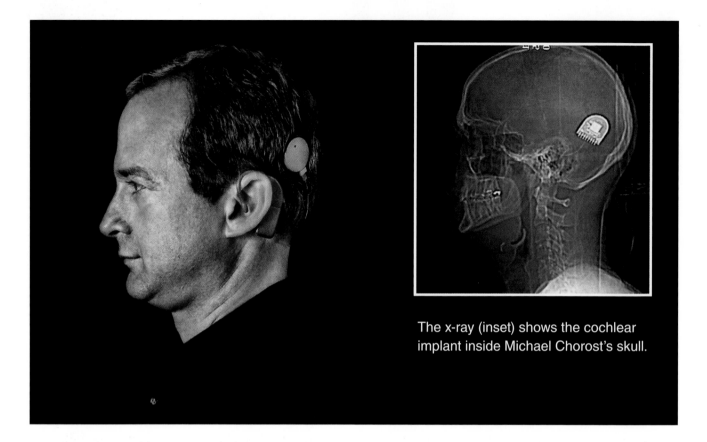

The x-ray (inset) shows the cochlear implant inside Michael Chorost's skull.

4   A more advanced type of bionic eye, called Argus II, was used for the first time by Larry Hester. A disease of the eye left Hester blind and in total darkness for over 30 years. But in September 2014, the 66-year-old was able to see again. The device consists of an implant in his left eye that connects his optic nerve to a pair of special glasses. When the device is turned on, it allows Hester to see light. Although his vision isn't completely restored, Hester can make out the shapes of objects, allowing him to see a world that had been in darkness for over three decades.

5   Some types of cyborg technology replace a lost ability by connecting directly to a person's nerves. Born partially deaf, Michael Chorost completely and suddenly lost his ability to hear in July of 2001. Two months later, doctors placed a cochlear implant, a kind of computer, inside his skull. This type of implant connects to auditory nerves and allows a deaf person to hear again. While Chorost's hearing isn't perfect, he continues to upgrade his implant as researchers improve the technology. Around the world, over 300,000 people have now been fitted with cochlear implants.

6   Steve Mann's cyborg technology changes an existing ability. In 1981, Mann, a researcher and inventor, created 36 kilograms (80 pounds) of wearable computer equipment that allowed him to change his reality. If Mann didn't want to see certain kinds of advertisements, his computer equipment would cover those advertisements with things that he actually wanted to see. So if he looked at a cigarette ad, for example, he would instead see an article that he wanted to read. In the 1990s, Mann reduced his computer equipment down to the size of a pair of glasses. Mann's device, the EyeTap, is now **permanently** attached to his head.

ARE WE ALL CYBORGS?

7   These examples of cyborg technology have enabled people to enhance or change their abilities and improve their lives. But does everyone want to **utilize** cyborg technology? It might be too late to decide. Cyborg anthropologist Amber Case argues that most of us are already cyborgs.

Steve Mann's cyborg technology—EyeTap—is permanently attached to his head.

8   Anyone who uses a computer or a smartphone, Case claims, is a cyborg. Consider the **data** that you have in your smartphone. It keeps information for you so you don't have to remember it: notes, phone numbers, email addresses, messages. It also allows you to communicate with friends and family via telephone, text messages, email, and social **networks** like Facebook, Twitter, Instagram, and Tumblr. Your computer and smartphone give you abilities that you would not otherwise have.

9   The potential benefits of cyborg technology are evident, but can this new technology be harmful, too? For example, when Steve Mann's EyeTap was forcibly **removed** at an airport, he had trouble walking and couldn't see correctly without it. The technology that had given him new abilities had apparently affected his abilities to walk and see. What might happen if, or when, more of us start to use devices like the EyeTap? Could we become too dependent on cyborg technology—and become less than human?

---

anthropologist: *n.* a scientist who studies people, society, and culture

auditory nerves: *n.* nerves that send sound information from the ear to the brain

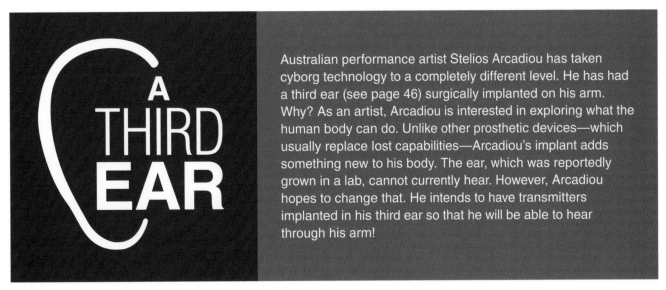

A THIRD EAR

Australian performance artist Stelios Arcadiou has taken cyborg technology to a completely different level. He has had a third ear (see page 46) surgically implanted on his arm. Why? As an artist, Arcadiou is interested in exploring what the human body can do. Unlike other prosthetic devices—which usually replace lost capabilities—Arcadiou's implant adds something new to his body. The ear, which was reportedly grown in a lab, cannot currently hear. However, Arcadiou hopes to change that. He intends to have transmitters implanted in his third ear so that he will be able to hear through his arm!

Australian performance artist Stelios Arcadiou shows off his third ear.

GETTING THE MAIN IDEAS

A. **Choose the best phrase to complete the first sentence of a summary of the passage.**

Cyborg technology _____.

   a. will someday help people enhance their natural abilities

   b. is helping people enhance their natural abilities

   c. has a few benefits but also many serious drawbacks

B. **Now complete the summary by checking (✓) the three sentences that best express the main ideas of the passage. The other sentences are either not main ideas or are not mentioned in the passage.**

   _____ **a.** Anthropologist Amber Case argues that computers and smartphones have turned most of us into cyborgs already.

   _____ **b.** The term *cyborg* today refers to a person who has mechanical body parts that improve his or her performance.

   _____ **c.** Born partially deaf, Chorost completely and suddenly lost his ability to hear in July of 2001.

   _____ **d.** Cyborg technology is already helping people—by compensating for abilities they have lost and by enhancing existing abilities.

   _____ **e.** Smartphones enhance our brains because they retain important information such as notes, phone numbers, email addresses, and messages.

UNDERSTANDING KEY DETAILS

A. **Use the information from the passage to write short answers to these questions.**

1. What device does Rob Spence's bionic eye contain? What does he use it for?

   _____

   _____

2. How is the bionic eye used by Larry Hester different from Spence's?

   _____

   _____

3. What human ability does Michael Chorost's device help him with?

   _____

4. What does Steve Mann's device do?

   _____

   _____

B. **Use the information in the section "A Third Ear" to write a short answer to this question.**

What does Stelios Arcadiou hope to do with his cyborg device?

   _____

   _____

CRITICAL THINKING

1. Analyzing. Amber Case says that we are already cyborgs. What examples does she give to support her idea?

   _____

   _____

2. Evaluating. Do you think that Case gives good examples of cyborg technology? Why or why not?

   _____

   _____

BUILDING VOCABULARY

A. Complete the information about bionics with the words in bold.

adapting   implant   mechanical   network   removed

Bionics is the study of _____ systems that function like living organisms or parts

1

of living organisms. Bionic parts have helped thousands of people improve their lives.

Here are some examples.

- Amanda Kitts lost her arm in a car accident. Doctors replaced it with a new, flesh-

  colored one. Underneath the plastic are three motors, a metal frame, and a(n)

  _____ of sophisticated electronics. When Kitts thinks about moving her arm,

  ₂

  sensors pick up impulses from her brain and turn motors to make the arm move.

- Aiden Keeney was born deaf. As a baby, he got cochlear implants in both ears. He is

  _____ well to his bionic devices. As a result, he has a good chance of

  ₃

  developing clear speech, his doctor says.

- Researchers are planning to develop an artificial hippocampus, the part of the brain that

  stores memories. They will _____ it in the brains of people with memory loss.

  ₄

While astonishing, it's worth remembering that not all of these devices work perfectly.

Some patients have had their bionic devices _____ because they interfere with

₅

other medical devices that the patients depend on, such as pacemakers (devices that

regulate the heartbeat).

Amanda Kitts is able to move her prosthetic arm using her mind.

B. **Match the bold words with their definitions.**

1. _____ Being able to hear changed Chorost's life **permanently**. His life has been different ever since he had a cochlear implant.

2. _____ Amanda Kitts is able to **utilize** her bionic arm in many of the same ways that she did with her natural arm.

3. _____ Modern smartphones hold an incredible amount of **data**. If we lost all our contacts and notes, we might feel very confused.

4. _____ A hearing aid is an example of an external **component** that helps a person hear.

5. _____ Someday, people may have bionic devices that help them move objects with their minds. This is an example of very **advanced** cyborg technology.

a. a part of something

b. raw or organized information

c. complex, difficult

d. to use

e. forever

GETTING MEANING FROM CONTEXT

Learning how to use the context—the surrounding words—to guess the meanings of unknown words helps increase your reading speed. It's also useful in situations where you do not have a dictionary, such as when you're taking a test.

Find the following sentence in the section "A Third Ear" on page 45. Then answer the questions below.

❝ Australian performance artist Stelios Arcadiou **has taken** cyborg technology **to a** completely **different level**. ❞

1. How is Stelios Arcadiou's ear different from the other devices you read about? Would you describe him as a "cyborg"? Why or why not?

_____

_____

2. What do you think the expression "to take to a new level" means?

a. To put something in a completely different place

b. To do something in a different or more advanced way

CRITICAL THINKING

Evaluating. Look again at the last paragraph of the passage. Could we become *too* dependent on cyborg technology, in your opinion? What are some possible drawbacks of cyborg technology? Discuss your ideas with a partner.

EXPLORE MORE

Read more about Amber Case's ideas at nationalgeographic.com/explorers. What does Case compare smartphones to? How does she describe the way people feel when they lose their smartphones? Share your information with the class.

TEDTALKS

I LISTEN TO COLOR

NEIL HARBISSON Artist and Cyborg Activist, TED speaker

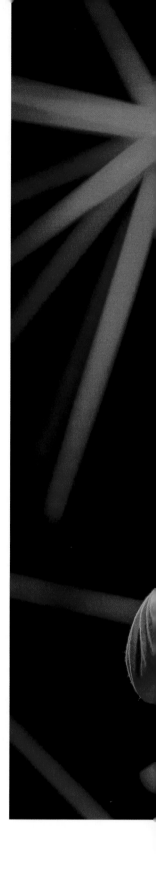

 Neil Harbisson was born without the ability to see colors. He explains, "To me, the sky is always gray, flowers are always gray, and television is still in black and white."

As a young adult, Harbisson studied music and art, and all his early artistic work was in black and white. Then a lecture on cybernetics gave him the idea for a device that would allow him to finally experience a world of color. The device, called the Eyeborg, matches colors with sounds. As a result, Harbisson is now able to create art using color.

Harbisson is now a cyborg activist. He created the Cyborg Foundation to help people who want to become cyborgs, to defend the rights of people with cyborg devices, and to promote cyborg research.

---

activist *n.* a person who works at changing something, especially in politics

In this lesson, you are going to watch segments of Harbisson's talk. Use the information above to answer each question.

1. Why was all of Harbisson's early artwork in black and white?

   _____

2. What does the Eyeborg match colors with? What did it enable Harbisson to do?

   _____

   _____

Neil Harbisson's **idea worth spreading** is that when we enhance our senses with cyborg technology, we can extend our knowledge of the world around us.

3. What do you think a "cyborg activist" is? In addition to art, what are some of Harbisson's interests?

_____

_____

TEDTALKS

PART 1

SOLVING A PROBLEM

PREVIEWING

A. **Read this excerpt from Neil Harbisson's talk. What verbs do you think are missing?**

❮❮ Well, I was born with a rare visual condition called achromatopsia, which is total color

blindness, so I've never seen color, and I don't know what color _____ like,
₁

because I come from a grayscale world. To me, the sky is always gray, flowers are

always gray, and television is still in black and white.

But, since the age of 21, instead of _____ color, I can hear color. In 2003, I
₂

started a project with computer scientist Adam Montandon, and the result . . . is this

electronic eye. It's a color sensor that detects the color frequency in front of me—and

_____ this frequency to a chip installed at the back of my head, and I
₃

_____ the color in front of me through the bone, through bone conduction. ❯❯
₄

---

color frequency: *n.* the number of light waves that pass a point in space in one second.
This number is different for each color.

(bone) conduction: *n.* moving through (bone)

B. **What do you think a "grayscale world" is? Discuss your ideas with a partner.**

_____

C. **Check your ideas above as you watch (▶) the first segment of the TED Talk.**

UNDERSTANDING KEY DETAILS

Complete the following sentences about the information in this part of the talk.

1. Harbisson's device helps him to _____.

2. When he first started using his device, Harbisson needed to remember the _____

   of colors and their _____.

3. When he started dreaming in color, Harbisson felt that the software and his _____

   had finally united and he started to feel like he was a _____.

UNDERSTANDING A PROCESS

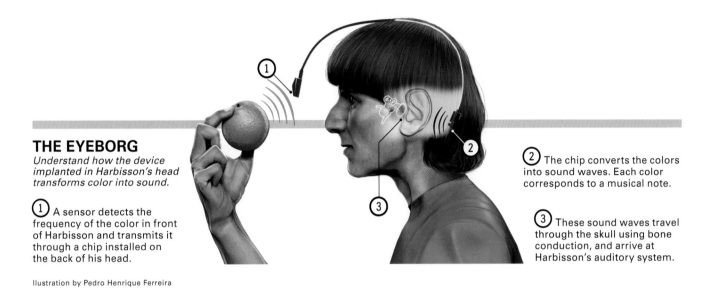

THE EYEBORG

Understand how the device implanted in Harbisson's head transforms color into sound.

① A sensor detects the frequency of the color in front of Harbisson and transmits it through a chip installed on the back of his head.

② The chip converts the colors into sound waves. Each color corresponds to a musical note.

③ These sound waves travel through the skull using bone conduction, and arrive at Harbisson's auditory system.

Ilustration by Pedro Henrique Ferreira

Study the infographic that shows how the Eyeborg works. Then complete the sentences.

Harbisson wears a sensor that sits in front of his head. The sensor connects to a chip that

is _____ in the back of Harbisson's head. The chip converts color frequencies
       1

to _____. The sounds that the chip produces _____ to his
       2   3

auditory nerves.

PART 2

A LIFE-CHANGING DEVICE

UNDERSTANDING KEY DETAILS

Watch (▶) the next segment of Harbisson's TED Talk. Use information from this part of the talk and the infographic on page 54 to complete the summary below.

Harbisson enjoys creating _____ of people. Instead of drawing someone's face,
                                    1

he points at them with the Eyeborg and writes down the different _____ he hears.
                                                                          2

Eventually, he was able to distinguish 360 _____, just like human vision. But
                                                    3

there were many more colors that the human eye could not detect. He decided to extend his

color senses, and added _____ and _____ to the color-to-sound
                                4   5

scale, so now he can hear colors that the human eye cannot perceive.

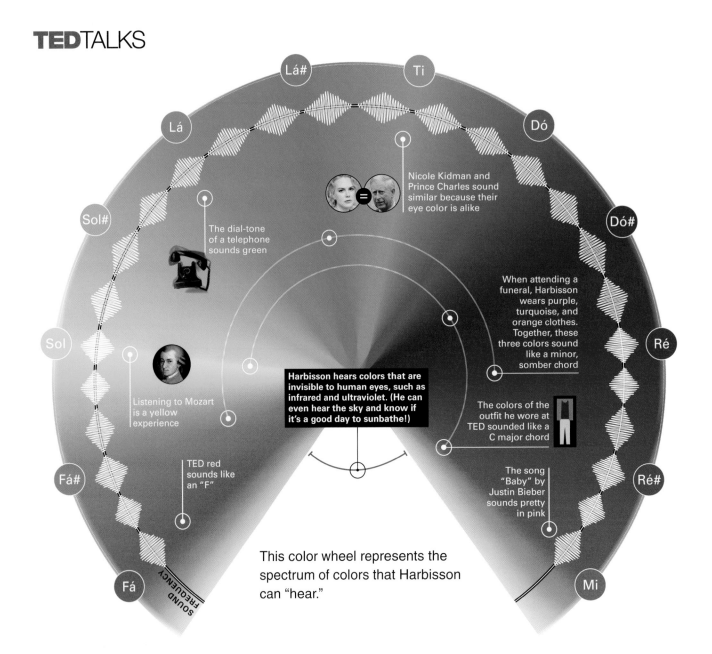

Lá#

Ti

Lá

Dó

Sol#

Dó#

Nicole Kidman and Prince Charles sound similar because their eye color is alike

The dial-tone of a telephone sounds green

When attending a funeral, Harbisson wears purple, turquoise, and orange clothes. Together, these three colors sound like a minor, somber chord

Sol

Ré

Harbisson hears colors that are invisible to human eyes, such as infrared and ultraviolet. (He can even hear the sky and know if it's a good day to sunbathe!)

Listening to Mozart is a yellow experience

The colors of the outfit he wore at TED sounded like a C major chord

Fá#

Ré#

TED red sounds like an "F"

The song "Baby" by Justin Bieber sounds pretty in pink

Fá

SOUND FREQUENCY

Mi

This color wheel represents the spectrum of colors that Harbisson can "hear."

CRITICAL THINKING

1. Reflecting. How do you think the Eyeborg improves Harbisson's life? What are some possible drawbacks to the Eyeborg?

_____

_____

2. Discussion. Think back to the types of cyborg devices that you read about in Lesson A. Which cyborg device is the most similar to Harbisson's? In what ways is it similar? Discuss your answer with a partner.

EXPLORE MORE

Find out more about Harbisson's device. Watch the rest of his talk at TED.com. What are some other ways his device affected his life and his work? Share your information with the class.

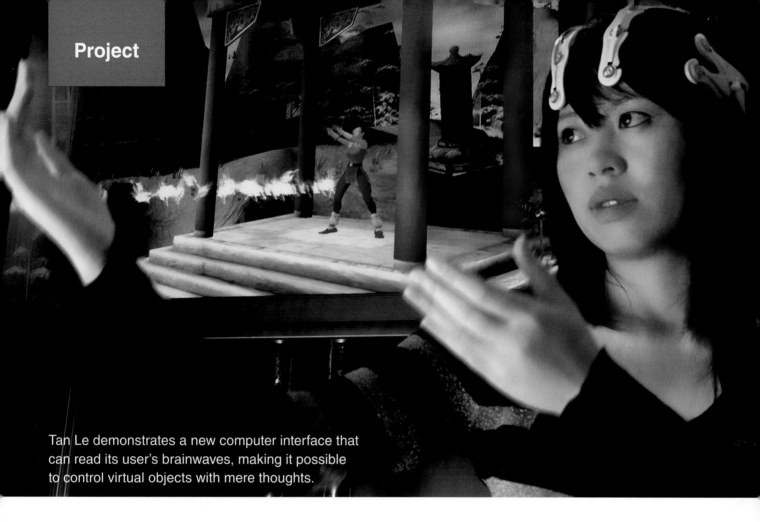

Project

Tan Le demonstrates a new computer interface that can read its user's brainwaves, making it possible to control virtual objects with mere thoughts.

A. Work with a partner. You are going to give a presentation on another example of cyborg technology.

1. Go to TED.com. Watch some of the following TED Talks to get ideas:

    - Tan Le, "A headset that reads your brainwaves"
    - Pranav Mistry, "The thrilling potential of SixthSense technology"
    - Hugh Herr, "The new bionics that let us run, climb and dance"
    - Eythor Bender, "Human exoskeletons—for war and healing"
    - Aimee Mullins, "My 12 pairs of legs"
    - Todd Kuiken, "A prosthetic arm that 'feels'"

2. With your partner, choose one of the devices in the TED Talks you saw or think of your own idea for a new cyborg technology. Answer these questions about it.

    - What is it made of? How does it work?
    - How is it connected to the body or the brain?
    - Does it replace or enhance an existing ability, or does it give a completely new ability?
    - How does it improve the user's quality of life?

3. Use your information to create a two-minute presentation. You can use drawings, photos, and video to explain your information.

B. Work with two other pairs.

- Give your presentations.
- As you listen, take notes.
- At the end, review your notes.
- Discuss: Which device is the most interesting? The most useful? Why?

EXPLORE MORE

Learn more about cyborg technology at nationalgeographic.com. Find out how scientists are using cyborg technology with animals and insects. Share your information with the class.

GOALS

IN THIS UNIT, YOU WILL:

- Read about different approaches to measuring progress.
- Learn about a new way of measuring global happiness.
- Explore how governments and other organizations can promote happiness.

THINK AND DISCUSS

1. What factors are important for happiness?

2. Do you think happiness is closely related to wealth? Why or why not?

HAPPY PLANET

Family members share a light moment as they clean and repaint their street in the Chefchaouen Medina, Morocco.

PRE-READING

A. Look at this scene from a science fiction movie and read the caption on page 59. Describe the scene. What does it say about our future?

_____

_____

_____

B. Look at the quote and introduction to the reading on this page. Note answers to these questions and discuss your ideas with a partner.

1. Why do you think Kennedy says that GNP is not a good measure of a nation's success?

_____

_____

_____

2. What other criteria can we look at when measuring a nation's progress? Check your ideas as you read the passage.

_____

_____

_____

GNP (gross national product): _n._ the total value of what is produced in a country within one year, used to measure economic growth

" . . . the gross national product does not allow for the health of our children, the quality of their education, or the joy of their play. It does not include the beauty of our poetry or the strength of our marriages . . . It measures neither our wit nor our courage, neither our wisdom nor our learning . . . it measures everything, in short, except that which makes life worthwhile. "

—Robert F. Kennedy

Why do we measure a nation's success by its productivity, rather than what really matters most to people? This reading, adapted from statistician Nic Marks's TED Talk, makes the case for a new definition of progress.

In the 2009 sci-fi movie *The Road*, adapted from Cormac McCarthy's novel, a father and son struggle to survive in a bleak future.

THE ROAD TO HAPPINESS?

1 What will the future be like? How will our actions today affect future generations? The answers to these questions are both fascinating and terrifying, especially as we glimpse the future in many science fiction movies. In one movie, *The Road*, we see a world where everything has been destroyed and there's nothing left of our **civilization**. A father and son are walking along the road, just trying to survive. Everything around them is **desolate**. It's just one example of the bleak future that cinema has imagined for us.

2 According to Nic Marks, this nightmarish vision of the future is one that many of those in the environmental movement have chosen to **promote**. According to him, environmentalists have focused on the worst-case scenario,

sending out warnings about all the negative **outcomes** that will emerge if we don't make **fundamental** changes to our behavior. Marks says we have focused attention on the problems, not on the solutions. "We've used fear," says Marks, ". . . when we're asking people to engage with our agenda around environmental **degradation** and climate change." Marks feels that this strategy is ineffective because fear tends to produce a fight-or-flight response. When an animal is frightened, it freezes and then runs away. Similarly, when people are presented with frightening scenarios of the future, they also freeze and run away.

WHAT IS PROGRESS?

3 Instead of focusing on this negative vision of the future, Marks asks, why not focus instead on how we can best improve our situation? How can we measure improvements in our global society so that we can **invest** our time and resources into building on those improvements? Marks believes that to do this, we first have to decide how we define *progress*. He believes economists and statisticians have provided the dominant definition of progress, and that this is a problem. Their definition assumes that if economic growth and gross national product (GNP) go up, life is going to get better. It assumes that our ultimate goal in life is to make more, earn more, and buy more.

4 In 1968, Robert Kennedy gave an eloquent **deconstruction** of the concept of gross national product. He concluded his talk by stating that the gross national product "measures everything, in short, except that which makes life **worthwhile**." Marks believes that if Kennedy were alive today, he would be asking statisticians to investigate what makes life worthwhile.

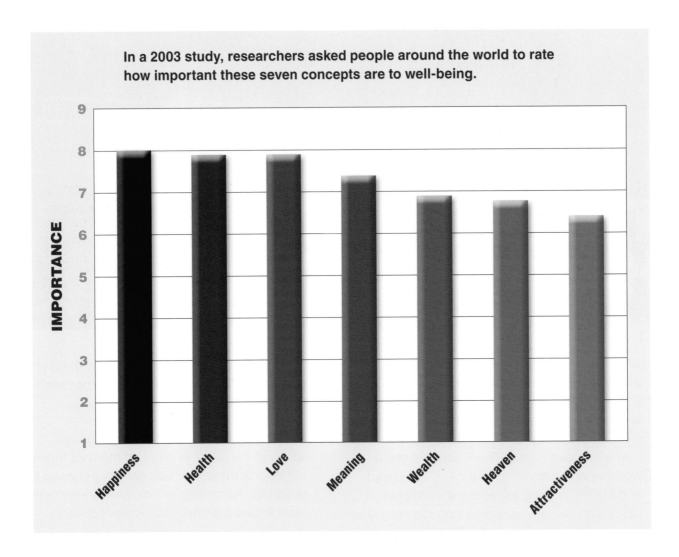

In a 2003 study, researchers asked people around the world to rate how important these seven concepts are to well-being.

A woman laughs as she slides down a ramp on a snowy day in Lanzhou, Gansu Province, China.

NEW PERSPECTIVES

5   Marks isn't alone in his beliefs; many social scientists are conducting research to ask people about what they want. One global survey, conducted by Ed Diener and Christie Scollon (2003), suggests that people measure their well-being very differently than most economists. Quite unsurprisingly, people all around the world say that what they want, or value most, is happiness—for themselves, their families, their children, and their communities. Money is important, but it's not nearly as important as happiness, love, or health.

6   We all want to be loved, and we all want to be healthy and live a full life. These seem to be natural human **aspirations**. Why are statisticians not measuring these? Why are we not thinking of the progress of nations in these terms, instead of just how much stuff we have? These are the important questions that Nic Marks believes will help us reach a better definition of progress.

---

agenda: *n.* a list of things to be done or considered

eloquent: *adj.* using language clearly and effectively

GETTING THE MAIN IDEAS

Use the information from the passage on pages 59–61 to answer each question.

1. What is the main idea of paragraphs 1 and 2?

   a. Filmmakers and environmentalists have very different views of the future.

   b. The world is probably heading for environmental disaster.

   c. Negative visions of the future are not helpful in changing people's behavior.

2. What is the main idea of paragraphs 3 and 4?

   a. Economists are now using a more effective way to measure progress in financial terms.

   b. We need to find a more useful way to measure progress in our global society.

   c. Measuring progress is challenging as there are so many definitions.

3. What was the main purpose of the survey mentioned in paragraph 5?

   a. To find out how important money is to happiness

   b. To find out how many people are happy

   c. To ask people what is important in their lives

4. What is the main purpose of the final paragraph?

   a. To suggest a different approach to measuring progress

   b. To persuade people to reduce the amount of stuff in their lives

   c. To explain why the environment is important to happiness

A group of boys having fun at a beach near the Angolan capital of Luanda

LINKING IDEAS

What are the contrasting viewpoints presented in the reading? Complete the summary with key ideas from the passage.

CONTRASTING VIEWPOINTS

Visions of the future

Definitions of *progress*

Negative

- focuses on _____ 1 ,

  not _____ 2

- discourages action

Positive

- focuses on how we can _____

  _____ 3

- invests _____ 4 into

  building on _____ 5

GDP

- _____ 6 definition only

- assumes our _____ 7 is

  to have more _____ 8

Alternative

- focuses on what _____

  _____ 9

ANALYZING AN ARGUMENT

A. **Use the information you noted above to write short answers to these questions.**

1. Why does Marks think that negative visions of the future are unhelpful?

   _____

   _____

2. Why does Marks feel the current definitions of progress are insufficient?

   _____

   _____

B. **What does the global survey tell us about what people consider most important? How does this support Marks's argument?**

   _____

   _____

UNDERSTANDING INFOGRAPHICS

A. Use the graph on page 60 to complete the summary.

In a 2003 study, Diener and Scollon asked people around the world which of the

_____ concepts they felt were most _____ in their life. _____
         1   2   3

ranked top of the list. _____ and love were equally important. Wealth is only in
                              4

_____ place.
      5

B. Discuss these questions with a partner.

1. What possible conclusions can you draw from this survey? What do you find most surprising?

2. How could cultural differences influence the results of this survey?

3. What further questions does the survey raise?

BUILDING VOCABULARY

A. The words in bold are from the passage. Circle the correct word to complete each sentence.

1. Nic Marks believes societies can **invest / aspire** more time and money into **promoting / aspiring** happiness.

2. Environmentalists are concerned about **deconstruction / degradation** of the environment.

3. The survey suggests that happiness is a universal **aspiration / outcome**.

4. Most people surveyed believe that love and health are more **worthwhile / desolate** than material wealth.

B. Use the context in the reading to match each word (1–5) to the best definition (a–e).

_____ 1. desolate   **a.** results

_____ 2. fundamental   **b.** uninhabited and bleak

_____ 3. outcomes   **c.** human society

_____ 4. civilization   **d.** significant; essential

_____ 5. deconstruction   **e.** examination; analysis

C. Discuss these questions with a partner.

1. What are your personal *aspirations* in life? How do they relate to Nic Marks's observations?

2. Which of the factors listed in the survey on page 60 do you think make life *worthwhile*? Why?

GETTING MEANING FROM CONTEXT

Note answers to the questions, and discuss your ideas with a partner.

1. Find this sentence in paragraph 2: " . . . environmentalists have focused on the worst-case scenario." What does "worst-case scenario" mean?

   _____

   _____

2. According to Marks, this negative vision is one that many of those in the environmental movement have chosen to promote (paragraph 2). What does "the environmental movement" mean?

   _____

   _____

3. Marks believes that a negative outlook produces a "fight-or-flight" response (paragraph 2). What do you think this means?

   _____

   _____

CRITICAL THINKING

1. Evaluating. Do you agree with Marks's view that too many movies portray the future in a negative way? Can you think of any exceptions?

   _____

   _____

2. Questioning. Identify two claims in the passage that you feel are doubtful or questionable. Explain why.

   Claim: _____

   _____

   Claim: _____

   _____

EXPLORE MORE

Read more about Nic Marks's ideas at www.nicmarks.org. What is the Happiness at Work survey? Share your information with the class.

TEDTALKS

THE HAPPY PLANET INDEX

NIC MARKS Statistician, TED speaker

 Nic Marks is a pioneer in the emerging field of well-being research.

Marks is particularly interested in promoting a balance between sustainable development and quality of life. To investigate this, he devised the Happy Planet Index (HPI)—a measure of human progress that takes into account not only how happy and healthy we are, but how efficiently we are using the resources of the planet.

The index uses international data on life expectancy, personal well-being (the happiness that people say they experience), and ecological footprint (a nation's impact on the environment in terms of per capita resource use):

$$\text{Happy Planet Index} \approx \frac{\text{Experienced well-being} \times \text{Life expectancy}}{\text{Ecological footprint}}$$

As Marks explains in his talk, "Economics is very interested in scarcity . . . and efficiency. It thinks in terms of how much bang do we get for our buck." Marks believes the HPI measure of progress goes beyond this narrow economic outlook and provides a true measure of global happiness levels.

---

efficiency: *n.* doing something without wasting resources

per capita: *n.* per person

scarcity: *n.* insufficient supply of something

(to get the best) bang for your buck: *n. (coll.)* to get the best value for your money

Nic Marks's **idea worth spreading** is that we need more meaningful measurements of national and global progress if we really want to improve our quality of life.

In this lesson, you are going to watch segments of Marks's TED Talk. Use the information on page 66, and the reading in Lesson A, to answer these questions.

1. How do you think the researchers measured the three components of the HPI?

   _____

   _____

2. How might a government try to increase its national HPI rating?

   _____

   _____

3. How do you think your country's HPI compares with other countries near you? Why?

   _____

   _____

PART 1

DEFINING HAPPINESS

PREVIEWING

A. **Look at the graph below from Marks's TED Talk. The colors represent certain groups of countries. Use the graph to complete the information.**

1. The vertical (Y) axis shows _____.

2. The horizontal (X) axis shows _____.

3. Countries in the Western world and the _____ have the highest ecological footprint.

4. Countries in _____ have low ecological footprints, but short happy life years.

5. Countries in _____ generally have the best balance of happy life years and low ecological footprint.

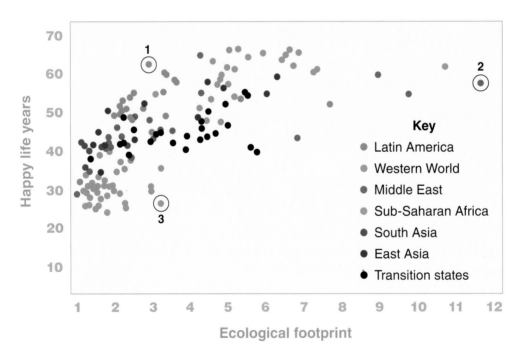

▲ **Happy Planet Index:** Happy life years and ecological footprint for 143 countries. Happy life years combine data on citizens' happiness and life expectancy.

B. **Which of the countries circled (1–3) do you think has the highest Happy Planet Index rating? What country do you think this is? Discuss your ideas with a partner.**

_____

IDENTIFYING KEY DETAILS

Watch (▶) the first segment of the TED Talk. Check your answers to the Previewing task. Then complete the summary below.

The country at the top left of the graph is _____. In this country, the average life
                                                    1

expectancy is _____ years, which is longer than in the U.S. According to the latest
                2

Gallup world poll, this is the happiest nation on the planet. And they use _____ of the
                                                                            3

resources that are used typically in the West. _____ percent of their electricity comes
                                                4

from renewable resources. . . . They abolished the _____ in 1949, and they invested
                                                    5

in social programs—health and education. They have one of the highest _____ rates
                                                                        6

in Latin America and in the world. And they have something else that is very important—

_____ connectedness.
   7

RECOGNIZING A SPEAKER'S MESSAGE

A. **Scan this excerpt from Marks's talk. What are the three levels he talks about?
Underline them.**

❝ [W]e need positive feedback loops for increasing well-being. At a government level,
they might create national accounts of well-being. At a business level, you might look at
the well-being of your employees, which we know is really linked to creativity, which is
linked to innovation, and we're going to need a lot of innovation to deal with those
environmental issues. At a personal level, we need these nudges, too. ❯❯

---

positive feedback loop: *n.* a process that enhances an effect by having an influence on the process that
created it

B. **Think of examples of actions that can be taken at each of the levels mentioned in
the excerpt. Discuss your ideas with a partner.**

_____

_____

_____

CRITICAL THINKING

Questioning. What factors are left out of the Happy Planet Index? If those factors were
included, how do you think it might affect the results? Discuss your ideas with a partner.

FIVE KEYS TO HAPPINESS

PREVIEWING

In the next part of his talk, Marks proposes five actions people can take to become happier. What do you think they might be? Note five ideas. Discuss your ideas with a partner.

RECOGNIZING MAIN IDEAS AND EXAMPLES

A. Watch (▶) the second part of Nic Marks's talk. Take notes on the five ways to increase well-being (or happiness).

Main Point	Example
1.	
2.	
3.	
4.	
5.	

B. Think of other examples to support each of his five ideas. Discuss your ideas with a partner.

CRITICAL THINKING

Applying. Which of Marks's five ideas would affect your life the most? Discuss your ideas with a partner.

EXPLORE MORE

Learn more about the Happy Planet Index by watching Nic Marks's full TED Talk at TED.com.

Project

An organic garden grown on the roof of a cooperative food store in Chicago, Illinois. Cooperatives like this cultivate a greater sense of social responsibility within the community.

A. Work with a partner. You are going to make a plan to help your community increase its sustainability and its citizens' happiness.

1. With your partner:
   - Choose one thing that could make the citizens of your community happier.
   - Choose one thing that would make it environmentally more sustainable.
   - Combine these two ideas into one plan.

2. Decide how the project could be funded and what benefits it would have.

3. Predict how the plan would affect different members of the community. Who would be in favor? Who would be against? Consider the perspectives of different groups.

4. Create a two-minute presentation. Include a timeline to show how the effects of your plan would develop over time.

B. Work with two other pairs. Give your presentations. As you listen to the other presentations, take notes on the following questions.

- Which suggestions would be easiest to implement?
- Which would have the farthest-reaching impact?
- What would be most cost-effective?
- Which of Nic Marks's five ideas does each plan address?

EXPLORE MORE

Watch Chip Conley's TED Talk "Measuring what makes life worthwhile" on TED.com. How do Conley's ideas about measuring happiness compare with those of Nic Marks? Share what you learn with your class.

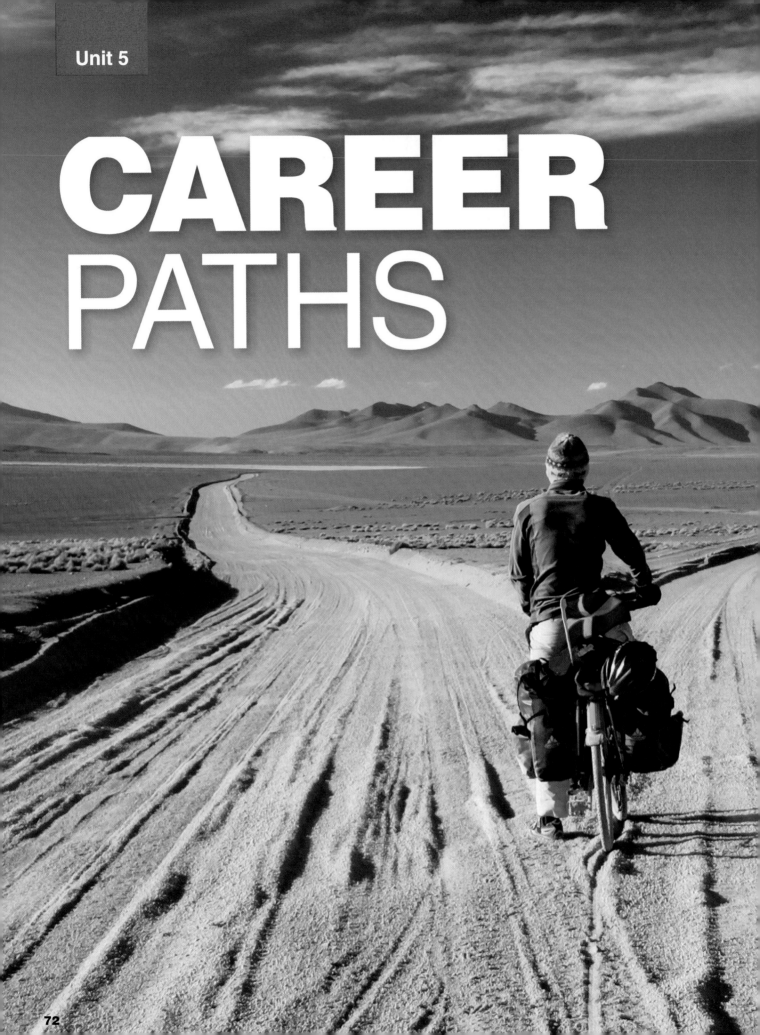

CAREER
PATHS

A cyclist traveling in Bolivia's Altiplano pauses to consider his direction.

GOALS

IN THIS UNIT, YOU WILL:

- Read about someone who took a mid-career break.
- Learn about the power of time off from work.
- Explore different approaches to time-off programs.

THINK AND DISCUSS

1. What is the best time in life to take a year off from work or school? Why?

2. For some people, the main purpose of work is to make money; for others, work gives joy or a purpose for living. What does the idea of "work" mean to you?

PRE-READING

A. Read the photo caption and the introduction to the reading on page 74. What might be the pros and cons of Winston Chen's decision to take a year off? Note your ideas in the tables below.

Pros

Cons

B. Scan the first two paragraphs on page 75 and answer the questions.

1. Which part of the world did he and his family move to?

_____

2. Who or what inspired them to make the change?

_____

C. Read the final paragraph on page 77. Was the family's experience positive or negative? Why do you think so?

_____

_____

A stormy day on Rødøy island, Norway. In 2011, Winston Chen left his job in the U.S. and came to this island to live with his family. In the foreground, Chen's daughter explores a deserted beach.

By **WINSTON CHEN**

MY YEAR IN THE ARCTIC

For most people, quitting your job to live for a year on a remote island is a distant fantasy. In this excerpt from his TED blog post, Winston Chen explains how he made that dream a reality.

1   Many people dream of the ultimate escape: throwing all the baggage of civilization away and taking off to live on a remote island. But few people—particularly professional couples with young kids—actually go through with it. And yet, that's just what my family did: We left Boston, and my **reliable** job at a software company, to go live on a tiny island north of the Arctic Circle for a year, unsure of what exactly we would do there or what we would face upon our return.

2   The seed of this idea was planted three years before, when a friend made me watch a TED Talk by graphic designer Stefan Sagmeister. He presented a tantalizing idea: "We spend about 25 years of our lives learning. Then there is about 40 years **reserved** for working. And then, tucked at the end of it, are about 15 years of retirement. I thought it might be helpful to cut off five of those retirement years and intersperse [them] in between those working years."

3   It struck a deep chord with me. I was an executive at a small software company, a typical management job where I spent the bulk of my working day in PowerPoint. I'd been working for about ten years, and felt like I was

---

intersperse: *v.* to place or mix something among other things

tantalizing: *adj.* tempting

75

Chen and his wife viewed the aurora borealis on February 14–Valentine's Day–2012: "The sky was not clear, but the northern lights were so strong that they lit up the clouds."

just going through the motions. We live in a society that celebrates strong work **ethics** and delayed gratification—all good things, but we've taken this cultural mindset to the extreme. We deny ourselves the time to do anything significant outside of work until we're **physically** and **mentally** well past our prime.

4 Ever since watching that talk, my wife and I wanted to take time off to go live in a faraway place. It took us three years to work up the nerve to actually do it. We finally decided to seize the moment when our children were old enough to remember the adventure, but not so old that they'd started elementary school. My wife, a teacher from Norway, was itching to get back into the classroom and found a teaching job at a small island in Arctic Norway called Rødøy. Our launch sequence began.

5 While Stefan Sagmeister's goal for his year off was to rejuvenate his creativity, mine was more loosely planned. I wanted to give myself a year without any concrete goals. I spent a lot of one-on-one time with our children with no objectives other than to be together. . . .

6 I hiked and fished. After dropping the kids off at the island school, I would carry on with my backpack and fishing rod and go off. I took photography more seriously, because I could afford the time to think about the picture rather than rushing just to capture something. I learned to play the ukulele and started to paint in oil after a long hiatus.

7 Three months into my island year, I rediscovered an old passion: programming. Just for fun, I started to develop a simple app that would read Web articles or PDF files out loud using synthesized speech. . . . I worked on developing it slowly but surely, and kept on with the other activities I was enjoying so much on the island, too. . . .

8 I think that people **hesitate** to make bold moves like the one my family did not because it's hard to leave: Leaving is actually the easy part. I think it's the fear of what happens after re-entry that keeps even the most adventurous families from straying far from home. When we headed home after a year, we had no jobs and no medical insurance waiting for us. And we

were immediately up against mortgage and car payments, plus all the costs of living in an expensive city.

9 But strangely, we felt truly at ease on our first evening back in the States as we sat on an outdoor patio with good friends talking about our respective summers. . . . Throughout that first evening of our return, I could feel palpable stress coming from our friends, a successful **couple** with substantial means. But my family, even with no **income**, felt at peace. That was when it dawned on me: Our island year wasn't just a memorable adventure. It had made us different people.

10 So many people who hear my story tell me how much they yearn for a similar experience: to take a big chunk of time off to **pursue** their heart's desire. To them I say: Have no fear. Most people are far more resilient to lifestyle changes than they think. And careers, which are rarely linear, can be just as resilient, too.

11 The upsides of taking a mid-career year of retirement are potentially life changing. By giving yourself time off and away, you're creating a climate teeming with possibilities. Perhaps you'll find passion in a new kind of work like I did. For sure, you'll come back with new confidence and fresh perspectives to fuel your career, plus stories and memories to **enrich** you and your family for life. And you won't have waited till you're 65.

Adapted from "Leave work for a year to go live on a remote island? How a TED Talk inspired me to take a mid-career sabbatical" by Winston Chen. Posted July 8, 2014: blog.ted.com

---

means: *n.* financial resources; income

mindset: *n.* a fixed way of thinking about something

palpable: *adj.* capable of being felt

rejuvenate: *v.* to make new or fresh again

resilient: *adj.* able to recover easily from difficulty

upsides: *n.* benefits

yearn for: *v.* to wish for; hope for

PREPARING FOR LAUNCH

Thinking of taking time off from your daily routine? Here are ten tips before you head off on your big adventure.

1. **Find inspiration:** Find out what others have done to make their time off a success.

2. **Plan ahead:** Start by listing interests and map out what you want to do with your time off.

3. **Set enough time:** Take at least three months off if you can.

4. **Save up:** Start deducting money from your paycheck to pay for your time off. Think of other ways to save, for example, by selling your car.

5. **Find support:** Investigate opportunities, such as fellowships, that generate income. Look for work opportunities overseas that can help finance your time off.

6. **Set expectations:** Tell friends and family about your plan, and ask them to help motivate you.

7. **Make a packing list:** If you're heading off for a whole year, think carefully about what you put—and don't put—in your backpack.

8. **Consider volunteering:** From wildlife conservation to helping businesses in developing countries, there are many options available.

9. **Learn a new skill:** Look for courses you could enroll in worldwide, from language classes to scuba diving.

10. **Travel the world:** A career time off is a great time to plan a long itinerary: the Trans-Siberian Railway, the Americas, Asia . . . the list is endless.

Sources: www.experteer-blog.com; www.wanderlust.co.uk/advice/career-breaks

GETTING THE MAIN IDEAS

The sentence below begins a brief summary of the reading passage. Complete the summary by checking (✓) the four sentences that state the most important ideas in the passage.

Taking a mid-career time off from work can rejuvenate your work life and your personal life.

1. _____ Winston Chen was inspired by a TED Talk to break away from the traditional mindset of working hard and waiting until retirement to take time off.

2. _____ Chen had worked for ten years at a software company in the U.S.

3. _____ Chen's time off revived his interest in programming and allowed him opportunities to spend more time with his family.

4. _____ Although they had to restart their lives when they came home, Chen and his family felt at peace.

5. _____ Chen concluded that although taking time off may seem risky, it has major benefits.

6. _____ Chen spent many days fishing while living on the island, as he had a lot of free time.

UNDERSTANDING SEQUENCE

A. **Read the sentences about Chen's experience. Use information from the passage to put them in the correct order (1–8).**

_____ a. Chen became more interested in hobbies, such as learning to play a musical instrument.

_____ b. Chen realized how much his time off from work changed him and his family.

_1_ c. Chen watched Stefan Sagmeister's TED Talk.

_____ d. Chen and his family returned to the U.S.

_____ e. Chen and his family went to Rødøy in the Arctic Circle.

_____ f. Chen and his wife decided to take a year off.

_____ g. Chen developed a new software application.

_____ h. Chen's wife applied for a teaching job on a small Norwegian island.

B. **Look at the advice under "Preparing for Launch" on page 77. Which of these do you think Chen's family did before they began their adventure? Discuss your ideas with a partner.**

UNDERSTANDING REASONS

Connect the reasons (a–f) with the events in Chen's life that resulted from them. Use the information in the passage to help you. One reason is extra.

a. Chen's wife wanted to work in a classroom again.

b. The year in Rødøy had a positive effect on the way they viewed their lives.

c. Chen had time to focus more on his hobbies on the island.

d. Chen believes many people think it's difficult to come back from a mid-career break.

e. They wanted to wait until their children were old enough to benefit from the experience.

f. Chen had been working for the same company for ten years and was beginning to feel bored with his job.

Event	Reason
A TED Talk about taking time off had a big impact on Chen.	
Chen and his wife decided to leave three years after watching the talk.	
The family chose to go to Rødøy, where a teaching job was available.	
Chen began to take photography more seriously.	
Chen and his family felt peaceful after they returned.	

UNDERSTANDING FIGURATIVE LANGUAGE

Figurative language includes words and expressions that go beyond their literal meaning. An example is "Our **launch sequence** began" (paragraph 4). Here, Chen is comparing the act of starting his year off with sending a spacecraft into the air.

A. **Find the following words and expressions in the passage. Think about the literal meaning of the bold words. (Check in a dictionary if you are unsure.) Then match each phrase with its meaning in the passage (a–g).**

1. _____ the **baggage** [of something] (para. 1)

2. _____ the **seed** of [this] idea was planted (para. 2)

3. _____ struck **a deep chord** (para. 3)

4. _____ **itching** to [do something] (para. 4)

5. _____ **concrete** goals (para. 5)

6. _____ **re-entry** (para. 8)

7. _____ **dawned** on me (para. 9)

a. having a strong desire

b. return from a trip

c. had a great impact or influence

d. the first inspiration occurred

e. the problems associated with something

f. made me realize something

g. firm plans or intentions

B. **Read the last paragraph on page 77 and answer the questions.**

1. What is the usual meaning of *fuel*? _Gas_

2. What part of speech (noun, verb, etc.) is it in this paragraph? _verb_

3. What do you think Chen means by "fuel your career"? _go ahead_

BUILDING VOCABULARY

A. **Complete the paragraph with the words below.**

enrich	ethic	hesitate	mentally	physical

At an average of 14 days per year, Americans have fewer vacation days than just about any other industrialized nation. Sociologists explain that this is due to a strong work

_____ in the culture. Americans traditionally feel that hard work is morally correct
  1

and that taking time off is a sign of laziness. Therefore, American workers often

_____ to ask for time off. It can be a difficult decision to make, as they worry that
  2

in their absence, a more industrious employee might take their place. However, experts

believe that taking time off from work can be _____ beneficial, for example, by
                                                3

helping you to clear your mind and to reduce your stress. It may also have _____
                                                                            4

benefits: People who take frequent breaks from work tend to suffer from fewer diseases.

Time off from work can also _____ people's work lives, as it gives them an
                              5

opportunity to explore new activities and ideas that they may be able to take back to

the workplace.

According to researchers, taking frequent time off from work can have significant health benefits.

B. Find the bolded words in the passage on pages 75–77. Read the words around them to guess their meanings. Then match the sentence parts.

1. A **couple** refers to _____

2. A person's **income** is _____

3. If you **pursue** something, _____

4. If something is **reliable**, _____

5. If something is **reserved**, _____

a. you work hard to achieve it.

b. it is held back for later use.

c. two people who are married or living together.

d. the money he or she earns from working or from investments.

e. it does what it's supposed to do and you can depend on it.

GETTING MEANING FROM CONTEXT

A. Find the following phrases in the passage. Use the context to match them with their meanings (a–g).

1. _____ going through the motions (para. 3)

2. _____ delayed gratification (para. 3)

3. _____ past our prime (para. 3)

4. _____ work up the nerve (para. 4)

5. _____ seize the moment (para. 4)

6. _____ up against (something) (para. 8)

7. _____ teeming with (para. 11)

a. develop enough courage

b. waiting for a reward in the future

c. facing something challenging

d. having a lot of (something)

e. doing things without thinking or feeling

f. take an opportunity (to do something)

g. not young anymore

B. Can you think of a time when you felt you were "going through the motions"? Describe the experience to a partner.

CRITICAL THINKING

1. Evaluating. Look back at your notes for Pre-Reading A on page 74. Which of those pros and cons does Chen mention? What other challenges do you think his family faced, either during or after their experience?

_____

_____

2. Interpreting. Winston Chen concludes that his year off wasn't "just a memorable adventure." He says, "It had made us different people." What does Chen mean by this? How do you think he and his family became "different people"? Discuss your ideas with a partner.

EXPLORE MORE

Read more about Chen's experience at blog.ted.com. Share what you learn with the class.

TEDTALKS

THE POWER OF TIME OFF

STEFAN SAGMEISTER Graphic Designer, TED speaker

Renowned for innovative album covers, posters, and a recent book of life lessons, designer Stefan Sagmeister has a unique way of looking at things.

Austrian-born Sagmeister began his career working for a youth magazine, and eventually went on to form his own design company in New York. He now provides a variety of creative services, from advertising to package design. His clients in the music, art, and scientific worlds include the Guggenheim Museum and the Rolling Stones. Paola Antonelli, senior curator at New York's Museum of Modern Art, describes Sagmeister as an "always surprising master of communication—the Johnny Depp of the design world."

As well as art and design, Sagmeister has a passionate interest in well-being and happiness. As he reported in a 2010 TED Talk, Sagmeister believes that factors like age, health, and climate have little to do with being happy; rather, our relationships with others are most important.

In this lesson, you are going to watch segments of Sagmeister's 2009 TED Talk. Use the information above to answer each question.

1. What kind of work does Sagmeister specialize in?

   _____

2. What has he learned about the nature of happiness? How does his view of happiness compare with Nic Marks's (in Unit 4)?

   _____

   _____

Sagmeister's **idea worth spreading** is that taking time off is actually good for our work, because it helps us approach it with a fresh perspective and new energy.

83

APPROACHES TO WORK

PREVIEWING

A. Chen's year in the Arctic was inspired by Sagmeister's talk. What information do you think the talk will contain? Discuss your ideas with a partner.

B. Look back at the quote from Sagmeister's talk on page 75 (paragraph 2). What does he think we should do with our retirement years? Check your ideas as you watch (▶) the first segment of the TED Talk.

UNDERSTANDING MAIN IDEAS

Why did Sagmeister decide to take time off from his design business?

UNDERSTANDING KEY DETAILS

A. Read the following excerpt. What are the three levels of work as defined by Jonathan Haidt? Underline three words.

❝ There is a fellow TEDster who spoke two years ago, Jonathan Haidt, who defined his work into three different levels. . . . I can see my work as a job. I do it for money. I likely already look forward to the weekend on Thursdays. . . . In a career, I'm definitely more engaged. But at the same time, there will be periods when I think, is all that really hard work really worth my while? While in the third one, in the calling, very much likely I would do it [even if I wasn't] financially compensated for it. ❯❯

B. Match each level you underlined above with one of these situations.

_____ a. Joey feels great happiness when he's at work. He would work at his profession even if he didn't get paid.

_____ b. Jen goes to work each day primarily because she needs to support herself. Most days at work, she's dreaming about her weekend activities.

_____ c. Sam feels engaged at work, but he often wonders if all his hard work has any real value.

CRITICAL THINKING

Synthesizing. Did Winston Chen have a job, a career, or a calling before he took time off? How do you think this changed after he took a year off?

THE SABBATICAL

PREDICTING

Read the excerpt from the next segment of Sagmeister's talk. Discuss your answers to these questions with a partner. Then check your ideas as you watch (▶) the next segment of the talk.

1. If you were going to go on a sabbatical for the first time, how would you approach it? Would you make specific plans? Why or why not?

2. How do you think Sagmeister approached his, and what happened as a result?

> 〝 In the beginning, on the first sabbatical, it was rather disastrous. I had thought that I should do this without any plan, that this vacuum of time somehow would be wonderful and enticing for idea generation. It was not. . . . [W]ithout a plan, I just reacted to little requests, . . . sending mail to Japanese design magazines and things like that. So I became my own intern. 〞

---

sabbatical: *n.* a period of rest, for professional and personal development

vacuum: *n.* a space with nothing in it at all

intern: *n.* a person who works for a business for little or no money in order to gain experience

UNDERSTANDING CAUSES AND EFFECTS

A. **Read the following excerpt about Sagmeister's first sabbatical. Then write short answers to the questions.**

> 〝 And I very quickly made a list of the things I was interested in, put them in a hierarchy, divided them into chunks of time and then made a plan, very much like in grade school. . . . Monday, 8 to 9: story writing; 9 to 10: future thinking. . . . And so on and so forth. And that actually, specifically as a starting point of the first sabbatical, worked really well for me. What came out of it? I really got close to design again. I had fun. Financially, seen over the long term, it was actually successful. Because of the improved quality, we could ask for higher prices. 〞

---

hierarchy: *n.* organization from higher to lower by importance

1. How did Sagmeister change his approach during his first sabbatical?

   _____

2. What was the effect of his approach?

   _____

   _____

UNDERSTANDING KEY DETAILS

Match details of Sagmeister's projects (a–f) to the locations (1–3).

a. spell out a message on a plaza

b. coins

c. animals and food items

d. bananas

e. a film on happiness

f. spell out a message on a wall

1. Bali: ____ ____   **2.** New York: ____ ____   **3.** Amsterdam: ____ ____

CRITICAL THINKING

1. Evaluating. Think about Sagmeister's examples of companies with innovative time-off programs. What are the possible advantages and disadvantages of programs such as these?

2. Personalizing. If you took time off from work every seven years, how would you use your time? How would you prepare for it? (For ideas, think back to the tips for "Preparing for Launch" on page 77.)

EXPLORE MORE

Find out more about Sagmeister's work and ideas on taking time off at TED.com. Share what you learn with the class.

Sagmeister's 2008 installation art in Amsterdam featured 250,000 Euro coins, arranged to spell out the sentence *Obsessions make my life worse and my work better.*

(To read the word, turn the page upside down)

Project

Comcast Cares Day is a day of community service organized by the companies Comcast and NBC Universal. Involving employees, families, and friends, it has become the U.S.A.'s largest single-day corporate volunteer effort.

A. Work with a partner. You are the owners of a company, and you are going to create a time-off program for your employees.

1. With your partner, decide the following:

   • What kind of company is it? For example, do you make things or do you provide services? What types of jobs do your employees have?
   • What is the purpose of your time-off program? Why do your employees need it?
   • Which employees will be able to participate in the program?
   • What kind of time-off program will it be? For example, will it be a sabbatical, a certain percentage of work time, a volunteer project, or some other kind of program?
   • What are other details of the program? For example, how much time will employees have off?
   • Will you expect anything from your employees, such as a report? Why or why not?

2. Create a two-minute presentation on your program. Prepare a chart that shows all the details of your program.

B. Work with two other pairs.

   • Give your presentations.
   • As you listen, take notes on the pros and cons of each program. At the end, review your notes.
   • Take a class vote. Which time-off program is the best? Why?

EXPLORE MORE

Check out the TED playlist "Work happier" on TED.com to learn about other ways that work life can be more fulfilling and productive. Share what you learn with the class.

TEXT
GENERATION

GOALS

IN THIS UNIT, YOU WILL:

- Read about the differences between spoken and written language.
- Learn about a new way of thinking about mobile texting.
- Explore how and why people text.

THINK AND DISCUSS

1. What are the main ways that you communicate with your family and friends?

2. How often do you text? Who do you text and in what situations?

A Sherpa in Nepal communicates with his family on his cell phone. With the development of mobile technology, we can now call and text from almost anywhere on the planet—even from very remote locations.

PRE-READING

A. Read the title and the introduction on page 90. Why might some people say texting is "the death of writing"?

_____

_____

_____

_____

B. Read the headings on pages 91–92. Discuss the following questions with a partner and note your ideas.

1. What do you think language is? How would you define it?

_____

_____

_____

2. How do you think speaking and writing differ? Make a list of the differences.

_____

_____

_____

_____

C. Look at the infographic on popular texting abbreviations on page 93. Which of these have you seen or used? Discuss your ideas with a partner.

THE DEATH OF WRITING?

Every day, people around the world send almost 50 billion text messages. This represents a major change in how people communicate with one another— and it's also having a significant impact on language itself.

A woman on a crowded train in Hong Kong connects with the outside world through her smartphone.

1 As text communication becomes faster and more commonplace, it has led to an array of space-saving abbreviations from IRL ("in real life") to JK ("just kidding"). Some people think these changes aren't for the best. As **linguist** John McWhorter says in his TED Talk *Txtng is killing language. JK!!!,* "we often hear that texting is a scourge; it spells the **decline** and fall of literacy, or at least writing ability, among young people . . . "

2 But McWhorter believes that texting isn't really writing. Rather, it's a new and unique form of communication.

WHAT IS LANGUAGE?

3 To understand McWhorter's ideas about texting, it's useful to take a look at what language really is. Human language is primarily oral. In other words, it is based in speech. McWhorter points out that while spoken language has existed for at least 80,000 years of human history, most experts agree that writing was invented only around 3200 B.C. He adds, "If humanity had existed for 24 hours, then writing only came along at about 11:07 P.M. That's how much of a latterly thing writing is."

4 Speaking is the fundamental **mode** of human communication. Children speak before they write. And while just about everyone learns to speak, not everyone learns how to write. McWhorter, in fact, describes writing as "a kind of artifice," a clever device that provided a new way to communicate.

---

latterly: *adj.* recent

WRITING VERSUS SPEAKING

5 How, then, do writing and speaking differ? The main difference, as McWhorter states, is that writing is a **conscious** process. Writing allows you to think deeply about ideas as you express them. It gives you the opportunity to evaluate, **expand on**, and **edit** your ideas more thoroughly than through speaking does. Writers use more words than speakers to express ideas. In addition, writers cannot get immediate **feedback** on their message; they don't know in the moment how well people have understood them.

6 Speaking, on the other hand, is more telegraphic than writing. In other words, speakers use fewer words to communicate a message. As McWhorter explains in his TED Talk, research shows that we speak in "word packets" of 7 to 10 words at a time. Speaking is also more **spontaneous** and less reflective. In addition, speakers can see in real time how well their listeners understand or are interested in their message, and they can correct or augment their message accordingly.

WRITE LIKE YOU SPEAK

7 While they are different forms of communication, writing and speaking influence each other, McWhorter says. An example is **formal** public speaking. Formal speeches follow the same structures and styles of written texts, but they are communicated orally. As McWhorter points out, the speechmaker speaks "in a certain way which has nothing to do with casual speech." In other words, it's not conversational; it's longer and more formal.

8 McWhorter concludes, "If you can speak like writing, then **logically** it follows that you might want to also sometimes write like you speak." This is where texting comes into the picture. Texting is a way to write like you speak. McWhorter points out that this wasn't really possible until technology made it easy to do. For example, compare typing on a typewriter or on a computer with the speed and ease of texting on a smartphone, not to mention the immediacy of the feedback from the recipient. The phones we have today allow us to write like we speak.

The Decline of Language?

While concerns about linguistic decline may seem like a modern phenomenon, people have actually been complaining about falling language standards for centuries.

An English professor in **1956** described students as not able to "write grammatically" or "read intelligently."

A **1917** teacher wrote, "Our freshmen can't spell, can't punctuate."

In **1871**, the president of Harvard University said bad spelling and "inelegance of expression in writing" were common among college students at the time.

In **63 A.D.**, a teacher complained about the way people were speaking Latin because they were simplifying it and not using its grammar correctly.

9 So, is texting a sign of linguistic decline? Not in McWhorter's opinion. He sees texting as a new and important form of discourse, "a miraculous thing," that allows us to expand our linguistic repertoire, much like writing did 5,000 years ago.

---

augment: *v.* to add to

come into the picture: *v.* to become relevant (to something)

discourse: *n.* spoken or written communication

inelegance: *n.* the state of not being polished, refined, or graceful

reflective: *adj.* having the qualities of deep thought

telegraphic: *adj.* short, missing unimportant words, like a telegraph message

SOME OF THE MOST POPULAR TEXTING ABBREVIATIONS

Abbreviation	Meaning
gtg	got to go
lol	laugh out loud
rofl	roll on the floor laughing
btw	by the way
sup	what's up?
fyi	for your information
asap	as soon as possible
w/	with
b4	before
l8r	later

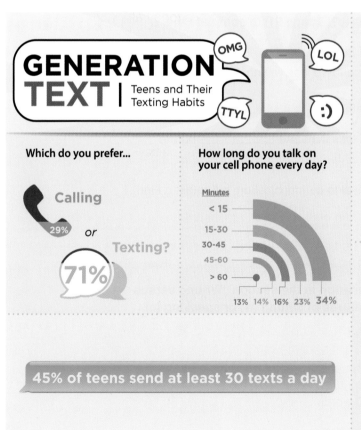

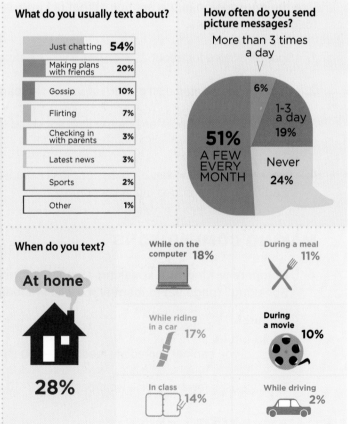

GETTING THE MAIN IDEAS

Complete the summary by checking (✓) the four sentences from the list that state the most important ideas in the passage.

Even though some people think texting is having a negative effect on people's written language, linguist John McWhorter thinks it is actually an entirely new way of communicating.

1. _____ Language is primarily oral, and writing is simply an additional means of communicating.

2. _____ People tend to write in groups of 7 to 10 words.

3. _____ Writing differs from speaking in that it is a conscious process, while speaking is more spontaneous.

4. _____ Writing and speaking can influence each other.

5. _____ Modern technology, such as smartphones, has facilitated our ability to write like we speak.

6. _____ Spoken language began roughly 80,000 years ago.

UNDERSTANDING KEY DETAILS

Use the information in the section "What Is Language?" (page 91) to complete the following statements.

1. Speech existed for about _____ years before there was writing.

2. Writing was invented a little over _____ years ago.

3. In McWhorter's 24-hour analogy, writing appeared less than one _____ before present time.

4. According to McWhorter, _____ isn't essential to communication, but rather a kind of artifice that we added much later on.

MAKING COMPARISONS

A. **Compare writing with speaking. Use the information in the section "Writing versus Speaking" (page 92) to identify if these are features of writing (w) or speaking (s).**

   Features

   a. _____ you can get immediate feedback—you can adjust your message quickly

   b. _____ uses fewer words—word packets of 7–10 words

   c. _____ feedback is delayed

   d. _____ reflective—you think about ideas as you express them

B. What other differences are there between speaking and writing? Note them in the T-chart below. Use information from the passage or your own ideas.

Speaking	Writing

UNDERSTANDING CONTRASTIVE LANGUAGE

Writers often mention contrasting ideas to make a point. These ideas are usually introduced with words such as *while*.

A. Find and underline four statements on pages 91–93 that use *while* to introduce contrasting ideas.

B. Choose the best paraphrase for each statement that you underlined in the passage.

Paragraph 3

a. Writing is a fairly new invention considering that humans have been speaking for at least 80,000 years.

b. Both written and spoken language are fairly new inventions, even though humans have been around for at least 80,000 years.

Paragraph 4

a. Nearly everyone learns to speak and write, but one form takes longer than the other.

b. Not everyone can write, but just about everyone can speak.

Paragraph 7

a. Although there are differences in how we speak and write, they are not as significant as you might think.

b. Speaking and writing are different forms of communication, but they have an important effect on each other.

The Decline of Language?

a. People have always been complaining about how communication is deteriorating, even though it seems like a very recent phenomenon.

b. It seems like people have always been complaining about how communication is deteriorating, but it's actually a very recent phenomenon.

BUILDING VOCABULARY

A. Complete the paragraph with the words below.

conscious	edit	formal	mode	spontaneous

Written English has both _____ and informal styles. The setting in which we write
and the audience for our writing determine the _____ we choose. For example,

academic settings are primarily formal, so, for the most part, an essay will have a

different style from an email to a friend. Informal writing—such as an email—is more

_____ than academic writing. We often write emails quickly without composing

them beforehand, and we often don't take the time to _____ them. On the other

hand, writing an academic essay is a much more _____ activity. For an essay, we

collect and examine ideas before writing, and we think carefully about how to organize

and develop them.

B. Choose the correct meaning for the words in bold.

1. Some people say that texting is an example of a **decline** in communication, but
    McWhorter thinks it's actually a clever advancement.

    a. rise   **b.** weakening

2. Since writers have the opportunity to **expand on** their ideas, they use more words
    than speakers.

    a. add details to   **b.** edit

3. Some writers are able to get a lot of **feedback** from readers through comments
    posted online.

    a. donations   **b.** responses

4. John McWhorter became interested in becoming a **linguist** at an early age, when he
    heard someone speaking a foreign language.

    a. person who studies the way   **b.** person who studies the structure
    children speak   of languages

5. If one purpose of texting is to communicate with others very quickly, then **logically** it
    follows that people will create abbreviations for certain expressions.

    a. reasonably   **b.** possibly

GETTING MEANING FROM CONTEXT

Look back at paragraph 1. Use the context to help you identify the meaning of the underlined words.

1. A <u>scourge</u> is something that causes a lot of _____ a group of people.

   a. trouble   **b.** happiness

2. An <u>array</u> of things or people is a _____ of them.

   a. large variety   **b.** limited number

3. To <u>spell</u> means to _____ that something will happen.

   a. signify   **b.** deny

CRITICAL THINKING

Interpreting. McWhorter says, ". . . texting . . . allows us to expand our linguistic repertoire." What do you think he means?

EXPLORE MORE

Learn how language has helped humans evolve by watching Mark Pagel's TED Talk "How language transformed humanity" at TED.com. Share what you learn with the class.

A sea turtle in an aquarium in Doha, Qatar, seems intrigued by a boy texting on his phone.

TEDTALKS

TXTNG IS KILLING LANGUAGE. JK!!!

JOHN McWHORTER Linguist, TED speaker

Does texting mean the death of good writing skills? John McWhorter thinks that there's much more to texting—linguistically, culturally—than it seems, and that it's all good news.

John McWhorter studies how language has evolved—and will continue to evolve—thanks to social, historical, and technological forces. One of his interests is texting, which he describes as an exciting new form of language.

So is McWhorter a fluent texter himself? When asked by an interviewer, McWhorter replied: "I don't text fluently. I'm 46 and the language I'm talking about came about in 2004, so I think I'm a little bit past the generation that would do it fluently." McWhorter relies on his students at Columbia University to help him understand the world of texting.

In this lesson, you are going to watch segments of McWhorter's TED Talk. Use the information above to answer each question.

1. What does McWhorter study?

   _____

   _____

2. How does McWhorter explain his lack of fluency as a texter?

   _____

   _____

On the slide:

atin, 63 A.D.

Spoken ... passel of words
consider ... en Latin, and the
gramma ... aking has broken
down. ... use anything but the
nominat ... ive ... it's gotten to the
point th ... tin is writing in what is
to them ... e, and it is an effort for
... it decently.

John McWhorter's **idea worth spreading** is that texting is not a scourge—it's a linguistic leap forward that's created a new form of communication between writing and speaking.

3. Based on what you read in Lesson A (pages 91–93), in what ways do you think texting could be described as a "new form of communication"?

_____

_____

TEDTALKS

"LOL . . ."

PREVIEWING

A. **Read this excerpt from John McWhorter's talk and answer the questions.**

❝ What texting is [. . .] is fingered speech. That's what texting is. Now we can write the way we talk. And it's a very interesting thing, but nevertheless easy to think that still it represents some sort of decline. We see this general bagginess of the structure, the lack of concern with rules and the way that we're used to learning on the blackboard, and so we think that something has gone wrong. It's a very natural sense.

But the fact of the matter is that what is going on is a kind of emergent complexity. That's what we're seeing in this fingered speech. And in order to understand it, what we want to see is the way, in this new kind of language, there is new structure coming up. ❯❯

---

bagginess: *n.* looseness; a state of not having structure

1. What is McWhorter's definition of texting? Underline it.

2. What concerns about texting does McWhorter mention?

   _____

3. What do you think McWhorter means when he says a "new structure" is emerging?

   _____

B. **Check your ideas as you watch (▶) the first segment of the TED Talk.**

UNDERSTANDING KEY DETAILS

Read this excerpt from McWhorter's talk and complete the notes below.

❝ LOL is being used [as] a marker of empathy. It's a marker of accommodation. We linguists call things like that pragmatic particles. Any spoken language that's used by real people has them. If you happen to speak Japanese, think about that little word *ne* that you use at the end of a lot of sentences. If you listen to the way black youth today speak, think about the use of the word *yo*. ❯❯

---

empathy: *n.* the ability to share or understand another person's feelings

accommodation: *n.* being helpful, cooperative

pragmatic particles: *n.* words, phrases, or sounds that don't have any meaning but make conversation easier

is used to show _____ ₁ and accommodation		is similar to "_____ ₃" in Japanese
is an example of a _____ ₂	**LOL**	is similar to "_____ ₄" used by black youths in the U.S.A.

100

"HAHA. SLASH . . . "

PREDICTING

A. Discuss with your partner what you think the purpose of the word *slash* is in this excerpt from the next part of the TED Talk.

Sally: So I need to find people to chill with.

Jake: Haha so you're going by yourself? Why?

Sally: For this summer program at NYU.

Jake: Haha. Slash I'm watching this video with suns players trying to shoot with one eye.

B. Watch (▶) the next segment of McWhorter's TED Talk. Was your answer correct?

APPLYING INFORMATION

A. Look at the underlined language markers in these conversations. Discuss what you think their functions are. Then match the markers with their functions (a–d).

_____ **1. Speaker 1:** What happened when you got your test results?

    Speaker 2: I was so surprised! I thought I was <u>like</u>, gonna die!

_____ **2. Speaker 1:** So, one way that people can augment their message is through facial expressions.

    Speaker 2: <u>Mm-mmm</u> . . .

    Speaker 1: For example . . .

_____ **3. Speaker 1:** You have to get one of these new phones! They're really worth the money.

    Speaker 2: <u>Well</u>, I don't know. Some reviewers say the older model works better.

_____ **4. Speaker 1:** James, where's your backpack?

    Speaker 2: <u>Oh</u>! Thanks! I almost forgot it.

a. Expresses surprise

b. Shows that the listener is paying attention

c. Softens the intensity of an extreme statement

d. Shows disagreement, degree of hesitation, or uncertainty

B. Share with the class some markers that have the same functions in another language that you know.

SUMMARIZING INFORMATION

Read the following excerpt from the TED Talk. Check (✓) four sentences that summarize the key points in this excerpt.

> " And so, the way I'm thinking of texting these days is that what we're seeing is a whole new way of writing that young people are developing, which they're using alongside their ordinary writing skills, and that means that they're able to do two things. Increasing evidence is that being bilingual is cognitively beneficial. That's also true of being bidialectal. That's certainly true of being bidialectal in terms of your writing. And so texting actually is evidence of a balancing act that young people are using today, not consciously, of course, but it's an expansion of their linguistic repertoire. »

cognitively beneficial: *adj.* helping with the functioning of the brain

bidialectal: *adj.* being able to use two different dialects (versions of languages)

_____ John McWhorter believes that texting may have some important benefits.

_____ Texting is a new form of writing being developed by young people.

_____ Being able to text well can help students improve their reading ability.

_____ Young people are now able to expand their range of writing abilities.

_____ Having more than one writing skill is good for the brain.

_____ Young people are getting better at writing while their other academic skills are declining.

CRITICAL THINKING

1. Evaluating. How well does McWhorter support his ideas? Can you think of any other arguments for or against texting? Note your ideas and discuss with a partner.

_____

_____

2. Personalizing. What are some ways that texting can go wrong or cause misunderstandings? Has this ever happened to you? Think of some examples and discuss with a partner.

EXPLORE MORE

Watch McWhorter's complete TED Talk at TED.com. How do you think language is going to change in the future? Share your ideas with the class.

Project

According to McWhorter, texting is a means for young people to expand their linguistic repertoire.

A. Work with a partner. You are going to find out how and why people text.

1. Collect examples of texts. Alternatively, you can write texts that you think are accurate examples of actual texts you have seen.

   Think about the following:

   • Why did the texter send a text instead of calling, emailing, or talking face-to-face?

   • What abbreviations does the texter use? What functions do they have?

   • Does the texter use *lol* or *slash*? If so, what functions do they have? Do they have the functions John McWhorter describes?

   • Does the texter use emoji/emoticons? If so, when and why?

2. Use your information to create a two-minute presentation. Print your texts and show them to the class as you present your analysis of them.

B. Work with two other pairs.

   • Give your presentations.
   • As you listen, take notes.
   • At the end, review your notes.
   • Discuss: Do the texts in the presentations support McWhorter's ideas? Did you learn any new functions for abbreviations or emoticons?

EXPLORE MORE

Find out more about how language changes by watching Anne Curzan's TED Talk "What makes a word real?" at TED.com. Share what you learn with the class.

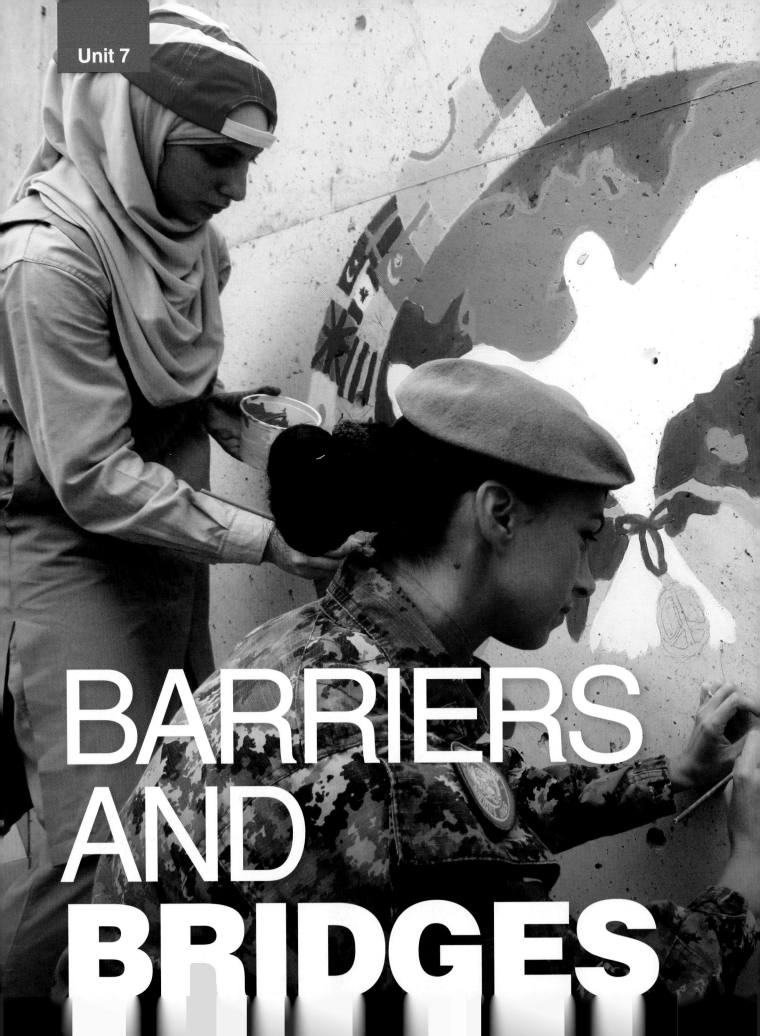

BARRIERS AND BRIDGES

UN Peacekeepers decorate a wall with symbols of peace.

GOALS

IN THIS UNIT, YOU WILL:

- Read about what one man learned at the 2014 World Cup Finals in Brazil.
- Learn about how we create perceptions of people who seem different from us.
- Explore how different people and cultures are portrayed in the media.

THINK AND DISCUSS

1. What are some ways you can learn about other countries or cultures?

2. How do you think people from other cultures perceive people from your culture? Why?

Lesson A

PRE-READING

A. **Think about a big sporting or entertainment event that you've been to. Answer the questions about the event.**

1. What was the atmosphere like? For example, was it friendly, hostile, or exciting?

   _____

   _____

2. Describe the other people who were at the event. For example, where did they come from? What language or languages did they speak?

   _____

   _____

   _____

3. Did you speak with any of the other people at the event? Why or why not? If you did, what was your experience like?

   _____

   _____

   _____

B. **Look at the headings in the reading on pages 107–109. What do you think the writer learned at the World Cup? Note your predictions and discuss with a partner.**

   _____

   _____

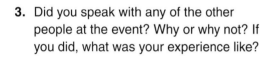 Aziz Abu Sarah, a Palestinian who grew up in Jerusalem, uses personal stories and cross-cultural education to promote peace and to bring people from different cultures together. The following reading passage is an adaptation of his *National Geographic* blog post titled "Why the World Cup Is About More Than Soccer," which he wrote while attending the 2014 World Cup Finals in Brazil.

Fans react during the Germany–Algeria match at the 2014 FIFA World Cup in Brazil.

BRINGING THE WORLD TOGETHER

A CHILDHOOD DREAM

1   In 1986, I watched my first soccer match on my parents' big box television, our family's first color TV that my father had purchased just for the event. I was six, and it was the World Cup final between Germany and Argentina.

2   Ever since then, I have dreamed of **attending** the World Cup, and soccer has been my favorite sport. This was partly because it was the only sport I could play, since there was no infrastructure for other games. All we needed for soccer was a ball and a street with limited traffic.

3   This year, I traveled to Brazil to make my dream of attending this international sporting event a reality. I was excited not only because I was at the World Cup, but also because I was in Brazil, the country that has won the cup more times than any other.

FRIENDS AND STRANGERS

4   The first match I attended was between Australia and Spain. Within minutes of walking into the stadium, I found myself surrounded by the excited buzz of other fans, talking and cheering together. Every now and then we hear about violence due to a soccer game, but

this match was mainly peaceful, except for one fight that **broke out** between a few people in my section of the stadium. Unlike what one normally sees on the news, which tends to broadcast images of vandalism and fighting, most of the fans in the stadium tried to **break up** the fight.

5   When the fight started, the whole section— thousands of people—began chanting with one voice, asking those fighting to stop. When they didn't, those same thousands of people—supporters of both teams—told the rabble-rousers to leave! Minutes later, they were escorted out of the stadium. Australian and Spanish fans refused to join a fight based on "nationalism" in sport. This is what sports should be about!

6   What struck me about the games I attended was the sense of camaraderie and sportsmanship, an atmosphere that is usually **ignored** on television in favor of stories about **isolated** outbreaks of violence. I met English, Australian, Algerian, Spanish, American, Russian, Lebanese, Argentine, and many Brazilian soccer fans, among others. Sometimes we were cheering for the same team and sometimes for opposite teams, but that didn't stop us from becoming friends. The stands were not divided between teams, and the interaction was often spirit-lifting.

7   I also watched the game in São Paulo that ousted Brazil from the World Cup. I was with friends at a large bar in the area, which hosted

THE WORLD'S GAME
The World Cup is the largest single-event sporting competition on the planet.

FOOTBALL IS TRULY GLOBAL

46.4%

of the world's population watched the 2010 FIFA World Cup in South Africa

Brazil, the 5th largest country in the world, could comfortably fit the hosts of the three previous World Cup Finals within its borders.

GERMANY

JAPAN

SOUTH KOREA

SOUTH AFRICA

2002 JAPAN–KOREA
The opening tournament of the 21st century was the first World Cup to be held in Asia.

2010 SOUTH AFRICA
It is estimated that almost half of the world's population watched the event, in over 200 countries.

2006 GERMANY
Over 715 million people around the world watched the final match, making it one of the most-watched events in television history.

2014 BRAZIL
Over 200 nations competed to take part, with 32 teams making it to the tournament in Brazil. 48,000 people attended the final game at the Maracanã Stadium in Rio de Janeiro; millions more around the world viewed the event live on television.

Source: www.fifa.com

Crowds in Kolkata, India, gather to watch a screening of a 2014 World Cup match.

a mix of Brazilian and German supporters. As Germany scored one goal after another, the sadness and even tears were visible on the faces of Brazilians. But German fans came to the Brazilians to comfort them! Other Brazilian fans were receiving text messages from German friends, **apologizing** that the game was ending with such a big gap. Everyone was hoping for the teams to play their best and for a good match.

BUILDING BRIDGES

8   What I love about the World Cup is it provides a chance for millions of people to learn about other countries and cultures. People learn about the countries of the teams they support and about their **opponents'** history, culture, and even some new phrases in a foreign language. This year's World Cup **coincides** with Ramadan, which is the month when Muslims abstain from eating and drinking from sunrise to sunset. Some players from Algeria, Nigeria, Germany, Belgium, and France were

fasting during their matches. Thanks to these Muslim players, millions of people learned about the **diversity** of these countries and about the religious tenet of fasting. Soccer is a game that not only gives people the chance to learn about each other but also has the **potential** to unite people.

9   Sports can be a dividing force, but the true spirit of sports is about unity, fun, and innovation. The matches at this World Cup have been exactly that so far, and I hope it remains so, because millions of children all over the world are watching these games and being inspired by what happens here in Brazil. It is amazing to me that the final game of this year's World Cup is between Argentina and Germany, a repeat of the first two World Cups I watched as a child!

---

fast: *v.* to abstain from all or certain foods, usually in observance of a holy day

tenet: *n.* main belief, or principle of a theory

vandalism: *n.* deliberate damaging of private or public property

GETTING THE MAIN IDEAS

Answer the questions.

1. What experience made Aziz Abu Sarah want to go to the World Cup?

   _____

2. What did Abu Sarah love most about his World Cup experience?

   a. Watching his favorite team win

   b. Learning about other cultures

   c. Attending the tournament's final game

3. Why does Abu Sarah think that soccer can bring people together?

   _____

UNDERSTANDING THE AUTHOR'S TONE AND PURPOSE

A. **What is the purpose of each section of Abu Sarah's article? Match each purpose below (a–d) with a heading from the reading. One item is not needed.**

   a. describes the surprising interactions among the people he met

   b. gives reasons that sports can have important benefits

   c. expresses how he felt when he met a famous soccer player as a young boy

   d. provides personal background information and explains his interest in the World Cup

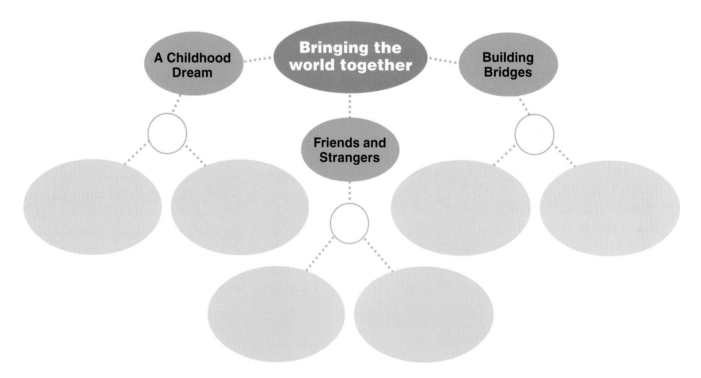

B. **Now complete the concept map above with two details from the reading that support each purpose.**

C. What is the author's overall tone, or attitude about his topic? Choose three words from the list below that describe his tone. Then find one detail from the reading that supports each of your answers.

critical	humorous	inspired	joyful
objective	optimistic	sad	sentimental

1. word: _____

   detail: _____

2. word: _____

   detail: _____

3. word: _____

   detail: _____

D. What do you think the main purpose of Aziz Abu Sarah's article is?

a. To report a factual story about some significant events that occurred during a trip to watch the World Cup in Brazil

b. To convince readers that they can't believe everything that they see on the news, especially stories about vandalism and fighting

c. To inspire people from different countries to use events such as the World Cup to learn about each other's cultures

BUILDING VOCABULARY

A. Complete the paragraph with the words below.

apologized   attending   diversity   opponent   potential

One of the most inspiring things that Abu Sarah witnessed while _____ the
                                                                    1
World Cup in Brazil was the way that soccer fans interacted with fans of competing

teams. For example, when Germany was scoring goal after goal against Brazil, German

fans were kind to fans of their _____. Instead of making fun of Brazilian fans
                                 2
because their team was losing, German fans _____ for the big difference in
                                            3
scores. The wide _____ of the fans, and their friendly behavior toward each other,
                  4
showed Abu Sarah that the international game of soccer has the _____ to bring
                                                               5
people together.

B. Choose the words that are closest in meaning to the words and phrases in bold. Use the context on pages 107–109 to help you.

1. **broke out**
   a. stopped   **b.** destroyed   **c.** started   **d.** lost

2. **break up**
   a. stop   **b.** injure   **c.** damage   **d.** report

3. **coincide**
   a. overlap   **b.** forget   **c.** differ   **d.** disagree

4. **ignore**
   a. notice   **b.** see   **c.** complain   **d.** disregard

5. **isolated**
   a. common   **b.** usual   **c.** rare   **d.** loud

GETTING MEANING FROM CONTEXT

A. Find each word or phrase (1–8) in the reading passage on pages 106–109. Use the context to help you understand the meaning. Then match each one with the best definition.

_____ **1.** infrastructure (paragraph 2)

_____ **2.** rabble-rousers (paragraph 5)

_____ **3.** struck me (paragraph 6)

_____ **4.** sense of camaraderie (paragraph 6)

_____ **5.** outbreaks of violence (paragraph 6)

_____ **6.** ousted (paragraph 7)

_____ **7.** abstain (paragraph 8)

_____ **8.** dividing force (paragraph 9)

a. surprised me

b. sudden occurrences of fighting

c. people who cause trouble

d. something that causes people to argue or disagree with each other

e. basic systems that are needed to make something work

f. forced to leave a place

g. feeling of friendship and trust between people who spend time together

h. refrain from doing something

B. What kinds of events, besides sports events, do you think are good for generating a sense of camaraderie? Note some ideas and share with a partner.

_____

_____

CRITICAL THINKING

Evaluating. According to Abu Sarah's article, what is shown on the news doesn't always accurately reflect the truth. Can you think of an example? Note some ideas and discuss with a partner.

a. What was the story you read or heard about in the news?

_____

_____

b. Why do you think the story wasn't really truthful?

_____

_____

EXPLORE MORE

Learn more about Aziz Abu Sarah (pictured below left) at nationalgeographic.com. Watch his TED Talk "For more tolerance, we need more . . . tourism?" at TED.com.

TEDTALKS

THE DANGER OF A SINGLE STORY

CHIMAMANDA NGOZI ADICHIE Novelist, TED speaker

🎧 Our lives—just like our cultures—consist of many overlapping stories, says award-winning writer Chimamanda Ngozi Adichie.

Many of Adichie's short stories and novels explore the legacy of colonialism in her native Nigeria and other African nations. Her characters—whether poor, middle class, or rich—are known for their dignity, and her descriptions of urban and rural communities are colorful and varied. Through these stories, Adichie effectively challenges the stereotypes that readers may have about modern-day Africa.

Adichie's work is contributing to a new wave of interest in contemporary African literature. Her recent novel *Americanah*—which describes the experience of a Nigerian woman who emigrates to the U.S.—was selected as one of the ten Best Books of 2013 by the *New York Times Book Review*. Her novel *Half of a Yellow Sun* was made into a movie in 2013 starring John Boyega, Thandie Newton, and Chiwetel Ejiofor.

---

colonialism: *n.* the practice of one country ruling another

dignity: *n.* self-respect

In this lesson, you are going to watch segments of Adichie's talk. Use the information above about Adichie to answer each question.

1. Where is Adichie from, and what does she write about?

   _____

   _____

Chimamanda Adichie's **idea worth spreading** is that we need to reject single stories about another country or people, or else we risk misunderstanding.

2. In what ways do you think she challenges readers' stereotypes?

_____

_____

3. How do you think her recent novel is different from her earlier work?

_____

_____

PART 1

WINDOWS TO NEW WORLDS

PREVIEWING

Read this excerpt from Chimamanda Adichie's talk. Why do you think the characters in Adichie's early stories were so different from her? Check your ideas as you watch (▶) the first segment of the TED Talk.

> « I was also an early writer, . . . all my characters were white and blue-eyed, they played in the snow, they ate apples, and they talked a lot about the weather, how lovely it was that the sun had come out. Now, this [was] despite the fact that I lived in Nigeria. I had never been outside Nigeria. We didn't have snow, we ate mangoes, and we never talked about the weather, because there was no need to. »

UNDERSTANDING KEY DETAILS

Use information from Adichie's TED Talk to answer these questions.

1. Where did the first books that Adichie read come from?

_____

2. Why did she read these books instead of African books?

_____

3. What did these books make Adichie believe about the characters in books?

_____

4. How did Adichie benefit from reading these first books?

_____

UNDERSTANDING A SEQUENCE OF EVENTS

Adichie's understanding of books changed when she was young. How did her understanding develop? Order the events in the flow chart.

a. Discovered African books

b. Gained a new understanding of literature

c. Wrote stories about characters like her

d. Read British and American children's books

e. Wrote stories about white, blue-eyed children

CRITICAL THINKING

Personalizing. **When you read books or watch shows or movies, do you prefer to read about and see people who are similar to you, or different from you? Why? What are some benefits in each case?**

CHANGING PRECONCEPTIONS

UNDERSTANDING A PROCESS

Adichie had preconceptions about a boy named Fide. Her ideas changed when she learned more about him. As you watch (▶) the next segment of her talk, complete the chart about her ideas and her new understanding.

Preconceived Ideas	Event That Changed Her Ideas	New Understanding
What did she assume about Fide's family?	What happened when she visited their home?	What did she realize about Fide's family?

IDENTIFYING MAIN IDEAS

A. **Use information from Adichie's talk to answer the questions.**

1. What did Adichie's roommate expect before she met Adichie? What surprised her about Adichie?

   _____

   _____

2. How is Adichie's roommate's reaction to her similar to Adichie's reaction to Fide?

   _____

   _____

   _____

3. Describe an instance in which Adichie was guilty of relying on a single story. What happened? What made her realize her mistake?

   _____

   _____

   _____

B. **Read this excerpt and answer the question below.**

❝ The single story creates stereotypes, and the problem with stereotypes is not that they are untrue but that they are incomplete. They make one story become the only story. . . . I've always felt that it is impossible to engage properly with a place or a person without engaging with all of the stories of that place and that person. The consequence of the single story is this: It robs people of dignity. It makes our recognition of our equal humanity difficult. It emphasizes how we are different rather than how we are similar. ❞

Why does Adichie believe that stereotypes are a problem? Give reasons using your own words.

_____ Stereotypes _____

_____

_____

CRITICAL THINKING

1. Synthesizing. In Lesson A, Aziz Abu Sarah described how attending the World Cup was a way to help counter cultural stereotypes. What might be some other ways? Discuss with a partner.

2. Relating. Think of a time when you made assumptions about someone and discovered that you were wrong. What did you learn about the person? How did you learn more about them? Describe the experience to a partner.

EXPLORE MORE

Find out more about Chimamanda Ngozi Adichie's experiences of overcoming "a single story" by watching her full TED Talk at TED.com

◀ A poster for the movie *Half of a Yellow Sun,* based on the novel by Adichie. The story examines the impact of war on the lives of five people in Nigeria during the 1960s.

Project

In the 2013 movie *The Lone Ranger*, actor Johnny Depp played the role of "Tonto," a Native American warrior.

A. Work with a partner. You are going to critically evaluate the portrayal of a character in a book, movie, or TV show.

1. With your partner, choose a story, book, movie, or TV show that presents a person from a particular culture.

2. Create a description of the character by answering the questions below.

   - What is the character's name?
   - What is the character's job?
   - Who are the character's friends?
   - How does the character dress?
   - How does the character speak?

   What are some of the character's other traits (e.g., hobbies, skills, favorite foods)?

3. Look at the answers you noted for the questions. Do they describe a realistic individual, a stereotype, or aspects of both?

4. Use your information to create a two-minute presentation explaining how that character is portrayed. You can use images and video to support your information.

B. Work with two other pairs.

   - Give your presentations.
   - As you listen, take notes.
   - At the end, review your notes.
   - Discuss: Do you agree or disagree with the ideas suggested in the presentations?

EXPLORE MORE

Chimamanda Ngozi Adichie says that you can't understand a whole culture based on a single story. But can you base a complex story on one picture? Watch Tracy Chevalier's TED Talk "Finding the story inside the painting" at TED.com. Share what you learn with the class.

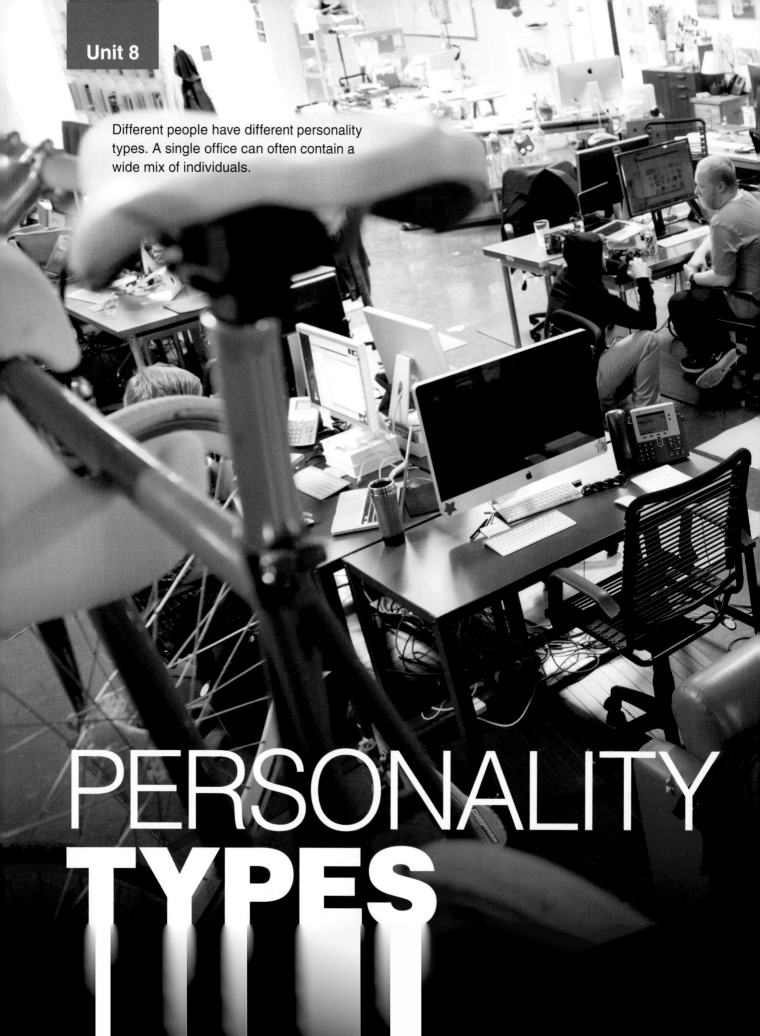

Different people have different personality types. A single office can often contain a wide mix of individuals.

PERSONALITY
TYPES

GOALS

IN THIS UNIT, YOU WILL:

- Read about one person's understanding of her own personality.
- Learn about attitudes toward and benefits of introversion.
- Explore some important contributions made by introverts.

THINK AND DISCUSS

1. What are some ways to describe someone's personality?

2. What kind of people do you think would like to work in the place shown on these pages? Why? How would you feel in this situation?

PRE-READING

A. Think about a time when you spent a lot of time with a large group of people. This might be a class trip, a trip with friends, a summer camp, etc. Answer the questions about your experience.

1. What did you expect before the experience? Did the experience meet your expectations? Explain.

_____

_____

_____

2. Who else was with you? Did you already know them or did you meet them for the first time?

_____

_____

3. What did you enjoy about your experience? What did you not enjoy?

_____

_____

B. The passage on pages 122–125 is an excerpt from Susan Cain's TED Talk, "The power of introverts." Read the first paragraph on pages 122–123. How do you think the author's expectations of summer camp compared with the reality? Share your ideas with a partner.

_____

_____

1   When I was nine years old, I went off to summer camp for the first time. And my mother packed me a suitcase full of books, which to me seemed like a perfectly natural thing to do. Because in my family, reading was the primary group activity. And this might sound antisocial to you, but for us it was really just a different way of being social. You have the animal warmth of your family sitting right next to you, but you are also free to go roaming around

A lone camper enjoys a quiet moment of solitude as she reads in her tent by a campfire.

THE IMPORTANCE OF SOLITUDE

the adventureland inside your own mind. And I had this idea that camp was going to be just like this, but better. I had a vision of ten girls sitting in a cabin cozily reading books in their matching nightgowns . . .

2 [O]n the very first day, our counselor gathered us all together and taught us a cheer that she said we would be doing every day for the rest of the summer to **instill** camp spirit. And it went like this: "R-O-W-D-I-E, that's the way

we spell rowdie! Rowdie, rowdie, let's get rowdie!" . . . I couldn't figure out for the life of me why we were supposed to be so rowdy, or why we had to spell this word incorrectly. But I recited . . . the cheer along with everybody else. I did my best. And I just waited for the time that I could go off and read my books.

---

rowdy: *adj.* rough, loud, and noisy

3 But the first time that I took my book out of my suitcase, the coolest girl in the bunk came up to me and she asked me, "Why are you being so mellow?"—mellow, of course, being the exact opposite of R-O-W-D-I-E. And then the second time I tried it, the counselor came up to me with a concerned expression on her face and she repeated the point about camp spirit and said we should all work very hard to be **outgoing**. And so I put my books away, back in their suitcase, and I put them under my bed, and there they stayed for the rest of the summer. I felt kind of guilty about this. I felt as if the books needed me somehow, and they were calling out to me and I was forsaking them. But . . . I didn't open that suitcase again until I was back home with my family at the end of the summer.

4 Now, I tell you this story about summer camp. I could have told you 50 others just like it—all the times that I got the message that somehow my quiet and introverted style of being was not necessarily the right way to go, that I should be trying to pass as more of an extrovert. And I always sensed deep down that this was wrong and that introverts were pretty excellent just as they were. But for years I denied this **intuition**, and so I became a Wall Street lawyer, of all things, instead of the writer that I had always **longed to be**— partly because I needed to prove to myself that I could be bold and assertive, too. And I was always going off to crowded bars when I really would have preferred to just have a nice dinner with friends. . . .

SHY OR INTROVERTED?

Although they may look similar, shyness and introversion are not at all the same.

An introverted person might also be shy, but shyness is a reaction to a fear of social judgment, while introversion is related to how a person responds to stimulation, particularly social stimulation.

According to Susan Cain,

"extroverts really crave large amounts of stimulation, whereas introverts feel at their most alive and . . . their most capable when they're in quieter, more low-key environments."

It's also important to note that while most people recognize themselves as one type of person or the other, no one is a pure extrovert or pure introvert.

As Cain explains,

"we all fall at different points . . . along the introvert / extrovert spectrum."

Steve Wozniak and Steve Jobs during the early development stages of the Apple computer

5 I made these self-negating choices so reflexively that I wasn't even aware that I was making them. Now this is what many introverts do, and it's our loss for sure, but it is also our **colleagues**' loss and our communities' loss. And at the risk of sounding grandiose, it is the world's loss. Because when it comes to creativity and to leadership, we need introverts doing what they do best. . . .

6 [W]hen **psychologists** look at the lives of the most creative people, what they find are people who are very good at exchanging ideas and advancing ideas, but who also have a serious streak of introversion in them. And this is because **solitude** is a crucial ingredient often to creativity. [Charles] Darwin . . . took long walks alone in the woods and **emphatically** turned down dinner party invitations. . . . Steve Wozniak invented the first Apple computer sitting alone in his cubicle in Hewlett-Packard where he was working at the time. And he says that he never would have become such an expert in the first place had he not been too introverted to leave the house when he was growing up. Now of course, this does not mean that we should all stop collaborating—and case in point is Steve Wozniak famously coming together with Steve Jobs to start Apple Computer—but it does mean that solitude matters, and that for some people it is the air that they breathe. . . .

7 This is no surprise, though, if you look at the **insights** of contemporary psychology. It turns out that we can't even be in a group of people without instinctively mirroring and mimicking their opinions. Even about seemingly personal . . . things like who you're attracted to, you will start aping the beliefs of the people around you without even realizing that's what you're doing. And groups famously follow the opinions of the most **dominant** or charismatic person in the room, even though there's zero correlation between being the best talker and having the best ideas. . . . You might be following the person with the best ideas, but you might not.

---

deny: *v.* to refuse to believe or acknowledge that something is true

guilty: *adj.* feeling that you have done something wrong

GETTING THE MAIN IDEAS

Use information from the reading to answer the questions.

1. What assumption did Susan Cain make after her experience at camp?

   a. At summer camp, you can do whatever you want to do.

   b. She should be more outgoing and less mellow.

   c. Most people enjoy the same things as she does.

2. According to Cain, why did she become a lawyer instead of a writer?

   _____

   _____

3. In later life, Cain felt that forcing introverts to act like extroverts is "the world's loss." What did she mean?

   _____

   _____

4. What connection does Cain make between introversion and creativity? What examples does she give to support this idea?

   _____

   _____

   _____

UNDERSTANDING SEQUENCE

A. **Cain describes the emotions she felt before, during, and after her experience at summer camp. Match each emotion with an event.**

   1. preparing to go to camp

   2. first day of camp

   3. being confronted at camp for being mellow

   4. after camp

   _____ confusion   _____ denial   _____ excitement   _____ guilt

B. **Underline the sentences in the passage that helped you identify each of Cain's emotional stages.**

UNDERSTANDING CLASSIFICATIONS

A. Read these descriptions of four individuals. Decide whether each person is more introverted (*I*), more extroverted (*E*), or shy (*S*), according to the information in the passage.

_____ 1. **Alex** lives with a roommate, although he doesn't know his roommate very well. Alex doesn't socialize very often—he'd like to make more friends, but he feels anxious about going to parties or conferences where he'll encounter new people. When strangers try to talk to him, he gets very nervous and worries what they will think of him. At work, he wants to contribute more in meetings, but doesn't feel comfortable and is often unsure what to say.

_____ 2. **Stephanie** has a large group of friends and is very social. She lives with three roommates, and is almost never alone. When she is alone, she feels like she's missing out on something. She enjoys hosting and attending parties. At work, she really looks forward to team meetings, whereas some of her colleagues are less enthusiastic.

_____ 3. **Paul** lives alone. He knows a lot of people and goes out with friends a lot, but he usually feels exhausted afterwards. He would like to spend more weekends at home alone, but when someone invites him to do something, he feels obligated to accept the invitation. He capably manages a large team of people at work, but is more interested in the tasks he can complete by himself.

_____ 4. **Karen** lives with her best friend. They have known each other for several years. In addition to her roommate, Karen has three or four other very close friends. She loves to spend time with them, going out to dinner, shopping, or just talking. However, after a long weekend of socializing, she likes to spend a few days at home alone. She doesn't usually lead meetings at work, but often shares ideas during meetings.

B. Complete the answers to the questions below with information from the reading passage.

1. What is the main difference between introversion and extroversion?

   Introverts need _____, and extroverts

   need _____.

2. What is the difference between shyness and introversion?

   Shy people _____, while introverted

   people _____.

C. Which of the people in Exercise A do you relate to most? In what way(s)? Discuss your answers with a partner.

BUILDING VOCABULARY

A. **Complete the paragraph with the words below.**

insight   outgoing   psychologists   solitude

What does it take to be a good leader? A lot of people might say that _____

1

people who are friendly and enjoy talking to others make good leaders. However, some

_____ believe that people who are quieter and spend more time alone might be

2

the best leaders. One reason behind this interesting _____ is that _____,

3   4

or spending time alone, allows many people to come up with creative ideas. Creative

problem solvers make good leaders.

B. **Match each word to the correct definition.**

a. colleagues   b. dominant   c. emphatically
d. instill   e. intuition   f. long to

_____ **1.** to make someone feel or believe something

_____ **2.** to want very much

_____ **3.** a feeling that something is true

_____ **4.** people that you work with

_____ **5.** with force

_____ 6. the most powerful or important

GETTING MEANING FROM CONTEXT

A. **Find each adjective below in the reading passage. Use the context to help you understand the meaning. Then complete each sentence with the correct word.**

antisocial   assertive   charismatic   grandiose   mellow

1. Someone who is _____ is calm and quiet.

2. If you are _____, you are confident about saying what you think.

3. If something is _____, it is bigger or more complex than it needs to be.

4. A(n) _____ person has a charming personality that people are attracted to.

5. A person who is _____ doesn't enjoy spending time with other people.

B. **Match each word or phrase (1–8) to the best definition (a–h). Use the context in the passage to help you understand the meaning.**

1. _____ for the life of me

2. _____ the right way to go

3. _____ deep down

4. _____ negating

5. _____ case in point

6. _____ the air that they breathe

7. _____ it turns out

8. _____ low-key

a. one example that illustrates the topic of discussion

b. the correct way to be

c. the most important thing to them

d. not even if I tried really hard

e. quiet, with a low intensity, restrained

f. at heart; internally

g. it happens to be true

h. denying the existence of (something)

CRITICAL THINKING

1. Inferring. According to Cain, introverts are often forced to be more extroverted, but rarely the other way around. Why do you think this is? Is this the case in your culture?

_____

_____

_____

2. Evaluating. Cain claims that there is "zero correlation between being the best talker and having the best ideas." Do you agree with this statement? Give examples to support your answer.

_____

_____

EXPLORE MORE

Read about the results of TED's poll "How introverted are you?" at blog.ted.com. What surprises you about the results? Do you think the TED Community is representative of society in general on this topic? Why or why not?

TEDTALKS

THE POWER OF INTROVERTS

SUSAN CAIN Author, TED speaker

🎧 With her book *Quiet: The Power of Introverts in a World That Can't Stop Talking,* Susan Cain has shone a light on the topic of introversion and its importance to society.

Cain is a former lawyer, an author, and a self-described introvert. In her book, Cain argues that while introverts have been seriously undervalued, they have made significant contributions to society. She also highlights the ways that schools, offices, and other institutions favor extroverts. Cain makes a case for a shift from a society that values extroversion to one that allows individuals to learn and work in environments that best suit them and best allow them to live up to their full potential.

Based on the popularity of her book and her TED Talk, it seems Cain isn't the only one who recognizes the need for an attitude change toward introverts. Cain's TED Talk has gotten more than 10 million views. Her book has been translated into 36 languages and was selected as the best book of the year by *Fast Company* magazine. In addition, she is working with an office design company to create office spaces and furniture that appeal to an introvert's need for quiet.

In this lesson, you are going to watch segments of Susan Cain's talk. Use the information above about Cain to answer each question.

1.   What do you think Cain hoped to accomplish by writing and publishing her book?

   _____

   _____

Susan Cain's **idea worth spreading** is that introverts are capable of great achievements, not in spite of their temperaments—but because of them.

2. Besides writing her book, what is one way that Cain is helping introverts to succeed?

_____

_____

3. How can we infer that many people share Cain's opinions about extroversion and introversion?

_____

_____

A BIAS TOWARD EXTROVERTS?

PREVIEWING

Read this excerpt from Susan Cain's talk and answer the questions below. Check your ideas as you watch (▶) the first segment of the TED Talk.

❝ When I was going to school, we sat in rows. We sat in rows of desks . . . and we did most of our work pretty autonomously. But nowadays, your typical classroom has pods of desks—four or five or six or seven kids all facing each other. And kids are working in countless group assignments. Even in subjects like math and creative writing, which you think would depend on solo flights of thought, kids are now expected to act as committee members. And for the kids who prefer to go off by themselves or just to work alone, those kids are seen as outliers often or, worse, as problem cases. And the vast majority of teachers report believing that the ideal student is an extrovert as opposed to an introvert, even though introverts actually get better grades and are more knowledgeable, according to research. ❞

---

autonomously: *adv.* alone and without help or interference from other people

outliers: *n.* people who are different from the majority of people

1. What do you think Cain means by the phrase "solo flights of thought"?

   _____

   _____

2. Why do you think that many teachers report that extroverts are ideal students, and introverts are "problem cases"?

   _____

   _____

3. How could the current classroom setups that Cain describes cause problems for some students?

   _____

   _____

UNDERSTANDING KEY DETAILS

Write answers to the questions using information from Cain's talk.

1. According to Cain, what percentage of people are introverts?

   _____

2. How is the world biased toward extroversion, according to Cain?

   _____

   _____

3. Why might introverted leaders be better than extroverted leaders?

   _____

   _____

CRITICAL THINKING

Personalizing. Have you experienced the types of classrooms and offices that Cain describes? If so, how did you feel? If not, how would you feel in these situations? Share your ideas with a partner.

_____

_____

Preschool students work at circular tables at Guangdong Country School, China.

PART 2

CHANGING ATTITUDES

UNDERSTANDING CAUSE AND EFFECT

According to Cain, Western societies, particularly the United States, used to favor introverts, but now favor extroverts. Watch (▶) the next part of Cain's talk and complete the chart below.

Introversion Was Valued	What Changed?	Extroversion Is Valued

• a culture of _____
              1
 	
 • role model: _____
 	
 _____
            2
	• evolved from agricultural economy to a
	
	    world of _____
	                       3
	
	 • people moved from _____
	                                4
	
	    to _____
	                 5
		• a culture of _____
		                   6
		
		 • role model: great _____
		
		 _____
		              7

UNDERSTANDING A SPEAKER'S MESSAGE

Complete the sentences below with information from the talk.

1. According to Cain, the world is facing enormous problems, and she believes that

   we should allow introverts to _____ so that they can come up

   with _____.

2. Cain is not confident with _____, so she prepares as best as she

   can. She is motivated to keep going by her desire to change _____

   toward introversion.

CRITICAL THINKING

Applying. Imagine that schools and businesses agree with Susan Cain's ideas. How might offices change? How might schools change? How might your own school be changed to be appropriate for a range of personality types? Discuss your ideas with a partner.

EXPLORE MORE

Take Susan Cain's "Quiet Quiz: Are You an Introvert or an Extrovert?" at thepowerofintroverts.com/about-the-book/quiet-quiz-are-you-an-introvert/.

Project

This famous photo by Margaret Bourke-White (1946) shows Mohandas K. Gandhi (Mahatma Gandhi) reading near a spinning wheel in his home.

A. Work with a partner. You are going to choose from a list of accomplished introverts and find out about their contributions.

1. With your partner, choose a famous introvert from the list below or find another example.

   - Albert Einstein
   - Lady Gaga
   - Mahatma Gandhi
   - Bill Gates
   - Audrey Hepburn
   - Angelina Jolie
   - Abraham Lincoln
   - Eleanor Roosevelt
   - J. K. Rowling
   - Emma Watson

2. Research and take notes on the following questions:

   - What are the person's accomplishments and/or contributions to society?
   - What are some examples of this person's introversion, for example, quotations from them, descriptions of their behavior, etc.?
   - What are some ways in which their introversion has helped—or hindered—their work?

3. Use your information to create a two-minute presentation. Use images or video to support your information.

B. Work with two other pairs.

   - Give your presentations.
   - As you listen, take notes.
   - At the end, review your notes.
   - Discuss: What new information did you learn? Did the presenters show a connection between the person's personality and his or her achievements? Which person do you want to learn more about?

EXPLORE MORE

Research online to find out about attitudes toward introversion/extroversion in different cultures around the world. Share your information with the class.

SMART
THINKING

A female chimpanzee in Gabon tries to reach behind a mirror.

IN THIS UNIT, YOU WILL:

- Read about current research on
  animal intelligence.
- Learn about a study of animal
  intelligence involving bonobos.
- Explore different types of intelligence

THINK AND DISCUSS

1. What are some ways in which animals
   communicate with each other?

2. What are some things that humans can do
   that animals can't? Do you think this means

Lesson A

PRE-READING

A. **Look at the photos and read the captions on pages 138–140. Discuss your answers to these questions with a partner.**

1. Which of these animals do you think is more intelligent? Why?

_____

_____

2. What other animal species do you think have high levels of intelligence?

_____

_____

B. **Why do you think researchers are interested in animal intelligence? What might be some possible benefits of studying this?**

_____

_____

_____

C. **Look at the title and headings in the reading passage on pages 139–141. How do you think animal intelligence, music, and the Internet might be connected? Note some ideas and share them with a partner.**

_____

_____

_____

A bottlenose dolphin paints with a paintbrush, as its trainer holds the artwork.

Are humans smarter than animals—or is our intelligence simply different from theirs? An innovative approach to communicating with other species may reveal some surprising answers.

138

THE NATURE OF INTELLIGENCE

1   The nature of human and animal intelligence has fascinated scientists and philosophers for centuries. In 1871, the naturalist Charles Darwin wrote in his book *The Descent of Man*, "There is no fundamental difference between man and the higher animals in their mental faculties. . . . The lower animals, like man, manifestly feel pleasure and pain, happiness, and misery." For Darwin, the difference between human and animal intelligence was one of degree and not of kind. He believed that other animals are **capable** of experiencing emotions, and have imagination as well as memory. Over generations, he argued, evolution naturally selects the more intelligent animals of each species, enabling each species to become more intelligent.

---

manifestly: *adv.* clearly; obviously

mental faculties: *n.* intelligence

An Asian elephant plays a xylophone at the Elephant Conservation Center, Thailand.

2 Others hold a **contrary** point of view: that human intelligence is fundamentally different. It has been claimed that no other species is capable of **abstract** thought, or has self-awareness. It has also been argued that other species are incapable of the complex linguistic systems through which we communicate ideas and express ourselves. However, the more we learn about animal intelligence, the more we begin to understand that animal intelligence may not be very different from ours; it may in fact be **superior** in specialized ways that our brains are not yet able to fully understand.

TALKING WITH DOLPHINS

3 Diana Reiss is a cognitive psychologist who studies intelligence in animals. Reiss has been teaching dolphins to communicate through an underwater keyboard of symbols that **correspond to** whistles and playful activities. Through this keyboard, the dolphins learned to perform activities on demand, and also to express their desire to perform them.

4 "What was **remarkable** was that they explored this keyboard on their own," she says. "They figured out how it worked. And they started to quickly imitate the sounds they were hearing on the keyboard." Reiss started to wonder about how to develop ways of communicating with other species—how to interact with them and learn about their intelligence. "How can we create interfaces, new windows into the minds of animals, with the technologies that exist today?" she asked.

THE LANGUAGE OF MUSIC

5 Reiss's work **resonated** with that of others working in different fields of arts and sciences. Peter Gabriel, a musician and composer, was **intrigued by** how animals understand music. "What was amazing to me was that [the animals] seemed a lot more **adept at** getting a handle on our language than we were at getting a handle on theirs," says Gabriel.

6 Gabriel has worked with a variety of musicians from around the world, often without any common language aside from music: "We sit behind our instruments and it's a way to connect," he says. Gabriel had heard about primatologist Susan Savage-Rumbaugh's research on communication with bonobos. He decided to try a similar approach by playing a keyboard with bonobos and found—amazingly—that they responded to music and were able to create musical compositions. He started to ask, "What would happen if we could somehow find new interfaces—visual, audio—to allow us to communicate with the remarkable beings we share the planet with?"

A NEW INTERNET?

7 This is a question that also intrigues Neil Gershenfeld, one of the founders of the Internet. Gershenfeld is particularly known for his work on "the Internet of Things"—the ability of computers or other electronic devices to communicate with each other via the Internet. But Gershenfeld believes communication between computers is not the only way forward. "We're starting to think about how you **integrate** the rest of the biomass of the planet into the Internet," he says.

8 Vint Cerf, another Internet pioneer, thinks animals can contribute to the Internet, too. He thinks it is important to learn how to communicate with other species. "These interactions with other animals will teach us, ultimately, how we might interact with an alien from another world," says Cerf, and thus potentially enable communication with intelligent life elsewhere in the universe. "I can hardly wait," he says.

---

biomass: *n.* all living organisms

cognitive: *adj.* relating to conscious mental activity

get a handle on: *phr.* start to understand something

on demand: *phr.* whenever asked to do something

pioneer: *n.* someone who is a leader in a particular area of research

primatologist: *n.* scientist who specializes in the study of primates (monkeys, apes, etc.)

SONGS OF THE HUMPBACK

Like many other marine animals, humpback whales use a variety of noises to communicate with each other. The three main types of sounds made by whales are clicks, whistles, and pulsed calls, probably produced by circulating air through the tubes and chambers of their respiratory system. The pulsed calls can last up to 30 minutes and, like songs, consist of several parts. Each male sings the same song over and over, and each whale in the group sings a slight variation of the same song. Whales in different geographical regions sing entirely different songs.

GETTING THE MAIN IDEAS

Match the beginning of each sentence (1–5) with the correct ending (a–e) to express the main ideas of the passage.

1. Darwin thought that other animals _____

2. Reiss discovered how dolphins _____

3. Gabriel found that he could use music _____

4. Gershenfeld thinks that we can use the Internet _____

5. Cerf predicts that communicating with animals _____

a. to interact with animals and cooperate on compositions.

b. could enable us to learn to talk with beings from other planets.

c. to connect all living things on our planet.

d. may experience the same emotions that we do.

e. can learn to use symbols to communicate with humans.

UNDERSTANDING KEY DETAILS

A. Scan the passage and note the paragraph(s) where the following questions are discussed.

_____ a. How might the Internet develop in the future?

_____ b. How does "the Internet of Things" work?

_____ c. How did the bonobos respond to the language of music?

_____ d. How is human intelligence different from animal intelligence?

_____ e. How did the dolphins learn new ways of communicating?

B. How do the songs of humpback whales resemble human language? How are they different?

_____

_____

C. Read paragraphs 3–6 again. Check (✔) all the answers that are true.

1. What did Reiss learn about dolphins in her research?

_____ a. They were able to understand symbols.

_____ b. They imitated whale songs.

_____ c. They used the keyboard to make requests.

_____ d. They responded to instructions from humans.

2. What did Peter Gabriel learn about bonobos?

_____ a. They were able to respond to music.

_____ b. They used music to communicate in the wild.

_____ c. They quickly learned to adapt their behavior.

_____ d. They could create some musical compositions.

INFERRING CONCLUSIONS

Writers often include quotations to imply further conclusions without directly stating them. What is implied by each of the following quotations?

1. Paragraph 4: "What was remarkable was that they explored this keyboard on their own," she says. "They figured out how it worked. And they started to quickly imitate the sounds they were hearing on the keyboard."

   a. Dolphins are more talented than humans at imitating sounds.

   b. Dolphins are able to work things out independently.

   c. Dolphins can understand a wide range of abstract concepts.

2. Paragraph 5: "What was amazing to me was that [the animals] seemed a lot more adept at getting a handle on our language than we were at getting a handle on theirs," says Gabriel.

   a. The animals adapted more easily than humans.

   b. Some animals were much better at communicating than others.

   c. The animals' linguistic ability was very basic compared to ours.

3. Paragraph 7: "We're starting to think about how you integrate the rest of the biomass of the planet into the Internet."

   a. The Internet has many technical challenges that we are currently unable to solve.

   b. The Internet doesn't include any biomass at all in its current form.

   c. The Internet could be expanded to link all living organisms.

Zoologist Jane Goodall and an infant chimpanzee reach out to touch each other's hands at the Gombe Stream National Park, Tanzania.

BUILDING VOCABULARY

A. **Choose the best definition for each phrase in bold.**

1. Animal brains may be **superior to** human brains in specialized ways.

    a. better than   **b.** larger than   **c.** similar to   **d.** close to

2. The underwater keyboard has symbols that **correspond to** whistles and playful activities.

    a. match   **b.** activate   **c.** express   **d.** include

3. Reiss's work **resonated with** that of others working in different fields of arts.

    a. ended with   **b.** cooperated with   **c.** corresponded with   **d.** conflicted with

4. Gabriel was **intrigued by** how animals understand music.

    a. inspired by   **b.** frustrated by   **c.** fascinated by   **d.** confused by

5. The bonobos were **adept at** learning to create music.

    a. not very good at   **b.** enthusiastic about   **c.** curious about   **d.** skilled at

B. **Complete the text with the words below.**

abstract	capable	contrary	integrate	remarkable

The idea that human intelligence is uniquely different from other animal species is being

challenged by recent research on animals. For example, many people believe that only

humans are _____ of being self-aware. _____ to popular belief, however,
  1   2

studies of dolphins and other animals have shown that many species of animals are able

to demonstrate self-awareness.

Another cognitive ability that was thought to be uniquely human is that of _____
  3

thought. Again, researchers have found that animals are able to manipulate symbols to

express ideas that are not concrete objects. Some species even seem to have

_____ skills and abilities that are superior to human abilities. An interspecies Internet
  4

could be a way to _____ various kinds of animals with each other and with humans.
  5

C. **Discuss these questions with a partner.**

1. Which of the communication methods discussed in the passage do you think is the most *remarkable*? Why?

2. Some people claim that animal intelligence is, in some ways, *superior to* human intelligence. Do you agree? Give reasons to support your idea.

GETTING MEANING FROM CONTEXT

Find the following sentence in the section "Talking with Dolphins" on page 140, and answer the questions below.

"How can we create *interfaces*, new windows into the minds of animals, with the technologies that exist today?"

1. What is the meaning of *interface* in this context?

   a. The surface where two things touch each other

   b. A way for two subjects to communicate with each other

   c. A way to connect two different computers together

2. How are *interfaces* like "new windows into the minds of animals"?

   _____

3. What are some examples of *interfaces* that you use for communication every day? Discuss your answers with a partner.

UNDERSTANDING REFERENCE

Pronouns are often used to refer to nouns previously mentioned in the text. In the excerpts below, what do the underlined words refer to?

1. For Darwin, the difference between human and animal intelligence was <u>one</u> of degree and not of kind. (paragraph 1)

   a. a difference   **b.** intelligence   **c.** a degree

2. Through this keyboard, the dolphins learned to perform activities on demand, and also to express <u>their</u> desire to perform them. (paragraph 3)

   a. the dolphins'   **b.** the activities'   **c.** the musicians'

3. "[the animals] seemed a lot more adept at getting a handle on our language than we were at getting a handle on <u>theirs</u>." (paragraph 5)

   a. the musicians'   **b.** the animals'   **c.** other people's

CRITICAL THINKING

Applying. The passage argues that we should explore more ways of communicating with animals. How could this impact our interactions with animals, for example, communicating with pets? Discuss your answers with a partner.

EXPLORE MORE

Learn more about the work of Reiss, Gabriel, Gershenfeld, and Cerf by watching their TED Talk, "The interspecies Internet? An idea in progress." What else has Reiss learned about dolphins? What is the interplanetary Internet?

TEDTALKS

THE GENTLE GENIUS OF BONOBOS

SUSAN SAVAGE-RUMBAUGH, Psychologist and Primatologist, TED speaker

🎧 Susan Savage-Rumbaugh's work with bonobos raises these questions: How much of what a species can do is determined by biology—and how much by cultural exposure?

Savage-Rumbaugh has spent much of her career investigating the cognitive and linguistic abilities of common chimpanzees and bonobos. Her research has shown that these animals are adept at picking up language and other types of behaviors generally considered to require a high degree of intelligence. Her work challenges our preconceptions about what characteristics can be considered uniquely human—such as causal thought or the ability to make tools. It also raises important questions concerning the skills and abilities that we consider to be human: if they are in fact the result of our social environment, and not the result of instinct or of innate biological traits.

---

causal thought: *n.* understanding the relationship between cause and effect

innate: *adj.* acquired from birth, not learned

trait: *n.* differentiating quality or characteristic

In this lesson, you are going to watch segments of Savage-Rumbaugh's TED Talk. Use the information above to answer each question.

1. What animals did Savage-Rumbaugh study? What did she want to find out?

_____

Susan Savage-Rumbaugh's **idea worth spreading** is that animals have the potential to develop astonishing skills given the right learning environment.

2. What kind of "human" behaviors do you think the bonobos in her study were able to learn?

   _____

3. Why do you think Savage-Rumbaugh's research challenges our preconceptions about being human?

   _____

TEDTALKS

PART 1

ALMOST HUMAN?

PREVIEWING

What traits do you consider to be uniquely human? Make a list and compare ideas with a partner.

UNDERSTANDING MAIN IDEAS

Watch (▶) the first part of the talk and answer the questions.

1. Susan Savage-Rumbaugh mentions four aspects of intelligence that people think are special to humans. What are they?

   causal thought _____ _____ _____

2. What five different activities of bonobos are shown in the TED Talk?

   a. Kanzi uses a _____ to _____.

   b. Kanzi's sister is learning how to _____.

   c. Kanzi's sister can recognize _____.

   d. Panbanisha uses _____ to cut Nyota's _____.

   e. Kanzi can make _____ from _____.

UNDERSTANDING A SPEAKER'S MESSAGE

A. **Complete the excerpts with the missing phrases. Then watch (▶) the segment again to check your answers.**

   1. Here Panbanisha uses scissors, ____, to groom Nyota.

   2. Realizing that Nyota might get hurt, Panbanisha, ____, carefully tugs to get the scissors back.

   3. Kanzi now makes his tools ____ may have made them two-and-a-half million years ago.

   4. Compare them to the tools our ancestors used; they ____ to Kanzi's.

   a. bear a striking resemblance

   b. instead of her hands

   c. just as our ancestors

   d. like any human mother

B. **What is the main message or idea that these phrases help to convey?**

   _____

LEARNING LANGUAGE

PREVIEWING

A. **Read the excerpt from the talk. What is the purpose of this research? What is Savage-Rumbaugh hoping to learn?**

> ❝ So we have a bi-species environment, we call it a "panhomoculture." We're learning how to become like them. We're learning how to communicate with them, in really high-pitched tones. We're learning that they probably have a language in the wild. And they're learning to become like us. Because we believe that it's not biology; it's culture. So we're sharing tools and technology and language with another species. ❞

_____

panhomoculture: *n.* pan (universal) homo (human) culture

_____

_____

B. **Check your ideas above as you watch (▶) the second segment of the talk.**

UNDERSTANDING SEQUENCE

Susan Savage-Rumbaugh describes how the bonobos are able to communicate with humans. Complete the summary with the words below.

communicate	draw	represents	shape	symbols	writing

The researchers are able to _____ with the bonobos using a set of _____, or
                                        1   2

lexigrams. For example, Panbanisha uses chalk to _____ an "A frame" pattern on the
                                                                3

floor. The _____ is similar to the lexigram on the keyboard that _____ a hut in
                    4   5

the woods. It shows that she is expressing a wish to go outside. In this way, Panbanisha is

able to use symbols—a form of _____ —to express her wishes.
                                              6

UNDERSTANDING KEY DETAILS

A. **Read this excerpt from the talk. Check (✓) three key points to acquiring language, according to Savage-Rumbaugh?**

❝ We found that the most important thing for permitting bonobos to acquire language is not to teach them. It's simply to use language around them, because the driving force in language acquisition is to understand what others, that are important to you, are saying to you. Once you have that capacity, the ability to produce language comes rather naturally and rather freely. So we want to create an environment in which bonobos, like all of the individuals with whom they are interacting—we want to create an environment in which they have fun, and an environment in which the others are meaningful individuals for them. ❞

For bonobos to acquire language, it's important to _____.

_____ repeat a few key words frequently

_____ praise them for using language

_____ use language around them

_____ teach them how to express themselves

_____ create a relaxed and fun environment

_____ interact with people who are important to them

B. **What's the difference between *acquiring* and being taught a language? Discuss with a partner.**

_____

_____

CRITICAL THINKING

Reflecting. How do Savage-Rumbaugh's methods compare with your experience of learning your first language? Give some examples of similarities and differences.

_____

_____

_____

EXPLORE MORE

View Susan Savage-Rumbaugh's full TED Talk on TED.com. What other activities of bonobos are shown? What do you think about the relationship between the researchers and the bonobos? Share what you learn with your class.

A Bornean orangutan, Siswi, saws a piece of firewood at the Tanjung Puting National Park, Indonesia.

A. **Work in a group of three. Imagine that you are going to apply for some research funding for a study of animal intelligence.**

1. In your group, select an animal species from one of the TED Talks listed below or identify a species on your own.

   - Deborah Gordon, "The emergent genius of ant colonies"
   - Denise Herzig, "Could we speak the language of dolphins?"
   - Jane Goodall, "What separates us from chimpanzees"

2. In your research:

   - decide why you think it's useful to study this species.
   - decide what you hope to learn.
   - decide how you plan to study it.

3. In your group, practice your presentation.

   - Decide who will present each part of the plan.
   - Make sure each person speaks for an equal amount of time.
   - Design a graphic organizer to use in your presentation.

B. **Present your plan to your class.**

1. Persuade your class that your research has the most benefits.
2. Answer questions from the class.

C. **Take a class vote on the best research plan.**

EXPLORE MORE

Find out more about animal intelligence by reading the article "This Is How You Study the Evolution of Animal Intelligence" on phenomena.nationalgeographic.com. What animals did the researchers study? What did they learn?

FACING FEAR

A daredevil cyclist performs a stunt jump off a cliff at Mineral Bottom Canyon, Utah, U.S.A.

GOALS

IN THIS UNIT, YOU WILL:

- Read about the risks and dangers of space missions.
- Learn about ways to deal with fear.
- Explore techniques for overcoming common fears.

THINK AND DISCUSS

1. What kind of risks or dangers do you face in your life?

2. What are some of the most dangerous occupations? What attracts people to them?

PRE-READING

A. What do you think are the most common fears or phobias? List three.

_____

_____

_____

B. Compare your ideas with the list on page 156. Do you know anyone who has these phobias?

_____

_____

_____

C. Look at the caption on page 155. What are some of the dangers of being an astronaut?

_____

_____

_____

_____

D. Skim the passage on pages 154–157. What central question does it address? Choose one option. Check your prediction as you read the passage.

a. What dangers do astronauts face?

b. How do astronauts deal with fear?

c. What safety equipment do astronauts use?

d. Why do astronauts choose a dangerous job?

KEEP CALM!

1 "Space is a harsh, inhospitable frontier and we are explorers, not colonizers," says astronaut Luca Parmitano. "The skills of our engineers and the technology surrounding us make things appear simple when they are not, and perhaps we forget this sometimes. Better not to forget. . . ."

Fear turns to panic as an astronaut detaches from her spacecraft following a space accident, in a scene from the 2013 movie *Gravity*.

2 You're an astronaut on a space station. You're suited up and about to go on a spacewalk to **conduct** experiments in space. What's the scariest thing that could happen?

3 **Detaching** from the spacecraft and getting lost in space? The sudden **malfunction** of all your breathing equipment? Losing consciousness due to the extreme heat inside your spacesuit?

4 Perhaps none of these can compare to the situation depicted in *Gravity,* the highly successful science fiction film directed by Alfonso Cuarón. In the movie, two astronauts are **stranded** in space. They have no way of contacting Earth, and have to overcome their fear in order to survive.

5 In real life, astronauts train for a range of life-threatening **emergencies** like these when they prepare for a space mission. The risks facing astronauts on a spacewalk range from a suit puncture (tiny shards of metal or rock can pierce their spacesuits and cause decompression) to a leaking helmet—something that actually happened to Italian

---

decompression: *n.* a reduction of pressure (for example, inside a spacesuit)

astronaut Luca Parmitano. When his helmet started filling up with water (probably because of a fault within the spacesuit's cooling system), his spacewalk had to be canceled. Parmitano was assisted by fellow crewmates back to the space station. When his helmet was removed, they found that it contained as much as two cups (half a liter) of fluid.

6   Another emergency that astronauts prepare for is accidental detachment from the spaceship. Astronauts go through **countless** hours of training for spacewalks to familiarize themselves with the route they will take after leaving the airlock. Spacesuits are also directly tethered to the space station. However, if a spacesuit does somehow detach, there is still a way back in—spacesuits all have mini-jetpacks that allow the spacewalker to get back to the station.

PREPARING FOR THE WORST

7   Given the **unpredictable** risks of space missions, how do astronauts train to deal with the feeling of fear? How do they stay calm enough to carry on in such extreme situations?

8   Chris Hadfield, former NASA astronaut and author of *An Astronaut's Guide to Life on Earth,* describes the importance of rationalization in **overcoming** fear. This involves asking questions about the logic of one's fear. Hadfield describes how repeated practice also helped him overcome his fear on space missions: "We knew everything there is to know about the spacesuit and we trained underwater thousands of times. And we don't just practice things going right, we practice things going wrong all the time."

9   Hadfield recommends a similar approach to overcoming more everyday fears. For example, if you have arachnophobia (a fear of spiders), you can research how many species of spiders in your immediate environment are likely to be poisonous (probably very few). In addition, repeated **exposure** to the feared situation or object can help to reduce your

10 COMMON PHOBIAS

What are people most afraid of? The following are ten of the most common phobias. These phobias can lead to symptoms such as dizziness, nausea, breathlessness, and, in extreme cases, panic attacks.

- Spiders
- Snakes
- Heights
- Closed spaces
- Illness or death
- Thunder and lightning
- Needles and injections
- Public speaking
- Flying
- Germs or dirt

Source: www.helpguide.org

fear. "Next time you see a spider web," Hadfield suggests, "have a good look—make sure it's not a black widow spider—and then walk into it. And then you see another spider web and walk into that one. It's just a little bit of fluffy stuff. It's not a big deal. And the spider that may come out is no more threat to you than a ladybug or a butterfly." If you walk through a hundred spider webs, says Hadfield, "you will have changed your fundamental human behavior."

▲ A female black widow spider. Arachnophobia (the fear of spiders) is one of the most common of all phobias.

MAKING FEAR YOUR FRIEND

10 This kind of strategy—known as exposure therapy—is an approach that many behavioral psychologists use when treating severe phobias. The process involves gradually and repeatedly exposing yourself to the source of your fear under safe and controlled conditions, often with a therapist to demonstrate and guide you along each stage of the therapy. Increasing familiarity with the source of your fear will help you to feel confident that it is **irrational**. Gradually, it will start to lose its power over you.

11 The key to the success of this technique is to start with situations that you find easy to handle and gradually work your way up to coping with more challenging situations (see "Climbing the Fear Ladder"). It can be effective for dealing with a variety of fears— from down-to-earth phobias such as a fear of dogs (cynophobia) and open spaces (agoraphobia) to coping with unlikely but potentially terrifying situations in outer space.

airlock: *n.* an airtight compartment with controlled pressure that separates the spacecraft from outer space

jetpack: *n.* a jet-powered backpack used by astronauts to move about independently in space

NASA: *n.* National Aeronautics and Space Administration; the U.S. government agency that is responsible for the civilian space program and space research

CLIMBING the FEAR LADDER

A FEAR LADDER is a list of steps that describe situations where you feel afraid or anxious.

FACING a FEAR of DOGS

The **FIRST STEP** is a situation where you feel only a mild anxiety.

After practicing the first situation under carefully controlled conditions until you feel calm and confident, you move on to the **NEXT STEP**.

STEP 10 Pet a larger dog off leash.

STEP 9 Pet a larger dog on a leash.

STEP 8 Pet a small dog that someone is holding.

STEP 7 Stand beside a dog on a leash.

STEP 6 Stand 5 feet away from a dog on a leash.

STEP 5 Stand 10 feet away from a dog on a leash.

STEP 4 Stand across the street from a dog on a leash.

STEP 3 Look at a dog through a window.

STEP 2 Watch a video with dogs in it.

STEP 1 Look at pictures of dogs.

EACH STEP increases the level of anxiety slightly so that you gradually adapt to more stressful situations.

By the time you reach the **TOP STEP**, you will be able to cope with situations that would have been extremely difficult for you at the beginning of the process.

Source: www.helpguide.org

GETTING THE MAIN IDEAS

A. **Choose the best two phrases to complete this first sentence of a summary of the passage.**

Astronauts learn to overcome their fear by _____ and by _____.

   a. testing jetpacks and safety equipment

   b. thinking rationally about risks and dangers

   c. practicing emergency situations many times

   d. creating and using a specific fear ladder

B. **Now check (✓) the three sentences that best express the main ideas of the passage.**

   _____ **a.** Astronauts can face many unpredictable dangers on space missions.

   _____ **b.** Astronauts are tethered to the spacecraft so that they won't float away.

   _____ **c.** Practicing dangerous scenarios can help astronauts to reduce anxiety.

   _____ **d.** Luca Parmitano's helmet started filling up with water, and the spacewalk was cancelled.

   _____ **e.** Many people are afraid of spiders and other wild animals.

   _____ **f.** Astronaut training has become much more challenging in recent years.

   _____ **g.** One way to reduce fear is to ask logical questions about the risks.

LINKING IDEAS AND EXAMPLES

Examples are used to illustrate main ideas and support the overall argument. One way to differentiate main ideas from details is to ask yourself if what you're reading is an example of a larger, more abstract idea.

Each of the following (1–3) is an example that illustrates a key idea (a–e) in the text. Match the examples with the ideas. Two ideas are extra.

1. Losing consciousness due to the extreme heat inside your spacesuit. (paragraph 3)

2. Spacesuits are directly tethered to the space station. (paragraph 6)

3. How many species of spider in your immediate environment are likely to be poisonous? (paragraph 9)

_____ **a.** A phobia that many people have

_____ **b.** A possible emergency in outer space

_____ **c.** A way to ensure safety and reduce risks

_____ **d.** How people react to fear

_____ **e.** Rationalization

CREATING A MAP OF THE TEXT

Complete the diagram with key points from the reading.

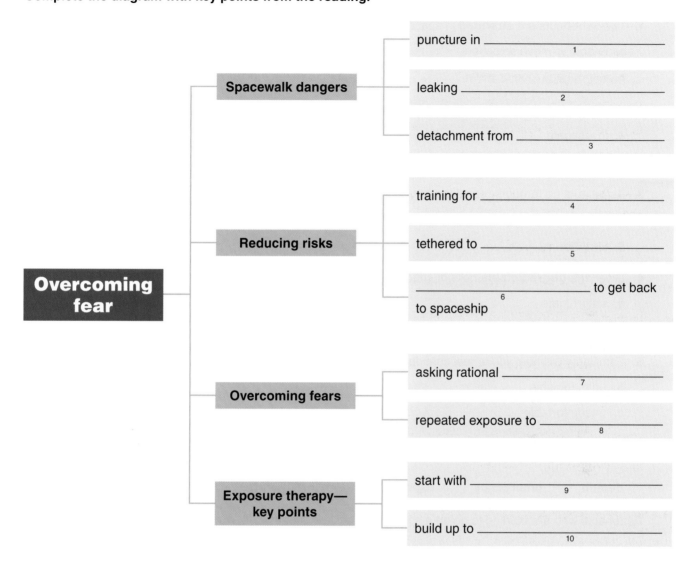

GETTING MEANING FROM CONTEXT

Use the context to help you complete the definitions of the words in italics.

1. Paragraph 5: "The risks facing astronauts on a spacewalk range from a suit *puncture* (tiny shards of metal or rock can pierce their spacesuits and cause decompression)."

   A *puncture* is a _____ made by a sharp object.

2. Paragraph 5: "The risks facing astronauts on a spacewalk range from a suit puncture . . . to a *leaking* helmet—something that actually happened to Italian astronaut Luca Parmitano. When his helmet started filling up with water, the spacewalk was cancelled."

   If something is *leaking*, it means that it has a hole or crack that lets _____.

3. Paragraph 9: "And then you see another spider web and walk into that one. It's just a little bit of fluffy stuff. It's *not a big deal.*"

   If something is *not a big deal,* it isn't very _____.

BUILDING VOCABULARY

A. **Choose the correct meaning of each word in italics.**

1. Two astronauts are **stranded** in space.

   a. unable to move anywhere

   b. very confused

   c. without any food or water

   d. separated from each other

2. You're about to **conduct** experiments in space.

   a. investigate

   b. repair

   c. solve

   d. perform

3. Astronauts go through **countless** hours of training.

   a. very many

   b. a fixed number

   c. very few

   d. regular

4. Given the **unpredictable** risks of spacewalk missions . . .

   a. unfortunate

   b. dangerous

   c. difficult to foresee

   d. difficult to describe

5. Familiarity will help you to feel confident that your fear is **irrational**.

   a. unimaginable

   b. unsuitable

   c. uncomfortable

   d. illogical

B. **Use the words below to complete the information about astronaut training.**

detach	emergency	exposure	malfunction	overcome

Astronauts who are training to go on a spacewalk must be prepared for any kind of

_____. There are many possible dangers, including a(n) _____ of their
    1   2

equipment, or the risk that they _____ from the spacecraft and float away into
                                    3

outer space. Astronauts must not only be prepared for these situations, they must also

be able to _____ their fear and stay calm so that they can complete their mission
            4

safely. Their training includes repeated _____ to emergency situations in similar
                                       5

conditions, for example, by training underwater.

UNDERSTANDING A PROCESS

Look at the infographic on page 157 and answer the following questions.

1. What is the purpose of the fear ladder?

    a. To identify what makes someone afraid

    b. To make fearful situations less frightening

    c. To help someone talk about their fear

2. How does each step help you to attain your goal?

    As you climb the fear ladder, each step _____

    so that you _____.

CRITICAL THINKING

1. Questioning. Look at the quote from Luca Parmitano at the beginning of the passage. Why does he say that "we are explorers, not colonizers"? What point is he trying to make? Discuss your answers with a partner.

2. Applying. Look back at your answer for Pre-Reading B. Do you think exposure therapy could help that person? Why or why not? Discuss your answers with a partner.

EXPLORE MORE

Learn more about the history of space exploration at: nationalgeographic.com/125/timelines/space-exploration/.

Russian cosmonaut Oleg Artemyev takes part in a preflight underwater training session in Moscow.

TEDTALKS

WHAT I LEARNED FROM GOING BLIND IN SPACE

CHRIS HADFIELD Astronaut, TED speaker

🔊 Chris Hadfield spent five months on the International Space Station (ISS)—including three as commander. During this time, Hadfield tweeted, blogged, and used other social media to share the wonders of space with a global audience back on Earth.

Now safely back on the ground, Hadfield continues to share the excitement of science and space travel, most recently in his book, *An Astronaut's Guide to Life on Earth*. As he says, "There are no wishy-washy astronauts. And whatever gave you the sense of tenacity and purpose to get that far in life is absolutely reaffirmed and deepened by the experience itself."

There's an astronaut saying: In space, "there is no problem so bad that you can't make it worse." So how do you deal with the complexity, the sheer pressure, of dealing with dangerous and scary situations? Hadfield has some ideas about how we can prepare for the worst in space—and life.

---

wishy-washy: *adj. (coll.)* indecisive, lacking clear ideas

tenacity: *n.* determination

In this lesson, you are going to watch segments of Hadfield's talk. Use the information above to answer each question.

1. What kind of personal qualities does Hadfield think are necessary to be an astronaut?

    _____

2. How do you think Hadfield "prepares for the worst"? Think about what you learned in the passage in Lesson A.

    _____

Hadfield's **idea worth spreading**
is that each of us can develop
effective techniques for overcoming
our fears.

PART 1

A RISKY VENTURE

PREVIEWING

Read the excerpt below from the beginning of Hadfield's talk. Check (✓) two things that we can infer from this excerpt.

> ❝ What's the scariest thing you've ever done? Or another way to say it is, what's the most dangerous thing that you've ever done? And why did you do it? I know what the most dangerous thing is that I've ever done because NASA does the math. You look back to the first five shuttle launches, the odds of a catastrophic event during the first five shuttle launches was one in nine. ❞

catastrophic: *adj.* disastrous

the odds: *n.* the probability of something happening

_____ **a.** Dangerous situations are not necessarily scary.

_____ **b.** Space shuttle missions are extremely dangerous.

_____ **c.** Many people do dangerous things and aren't scared.

_____ **d.** Hadfield has been on more shuttle launches than anyone else.

_____ **e.** There isn't anything more dangerous than flying a space shuttle.

_____ **f.** Traveling in a space shuttle was the most dangerous thing Hadfield has done.

UNDERSTANDING MAIN IDEAS

Watch (▶) the first part of Hadfield's talk, and answer the questions.

1. When and how was Hadfield inspired to become an astronaut?

   _____

   _____

2. According to Hadfield, what is the most amazing experience for an astronaut?

   _____

   _____

3. How did Hadfield's experiences change his perspective?

   _____

   _____

INTERPRETING DESCRIPTIONS

A. Hadfield uses some dramatic visual imagery to convey the emotional and sensory impact of his experiences. What is he describing in these excerpts? Match the descriptions with the things they describe.

a. "You are in the grip of something that is vastly more powerful than yourself. It's shaking you so hard, you can't focus on the instruments in front of you. It's like you're in the jaws of some enormous dog . . . "

b. "You get lighter and lighter, the force gets . . . heavier and heavier. It feels like someone's pouring cement on you or something."

c. " . . . a million-pound creation that's going around the world at five miles a second, eight kilometers a second, around the world 16 times a day, . . . "

d. " . . . the turning orb [is] like a self-propelled art gallery of fantastic, constantly changing beauty . . . It's roaring silently with color and texture as it pours by mesmerizingly next to you . . . "

e. " . . . an entirely different perspective, you're not looking up at the universe, you and the Earth are going through the universe together. And you're holding on with one hand, looking at the world turn beside you."

f. "unfathomable blackness, with a texture you feel like you could stick your hand into."

_____ the view of Earth from space

_____ the experience of taking a spacewalk

_____ the International Space Station

_____ being inside a rocket as it starts to lift off

_____ the view of deep space from outside the spacecraft

_____ feeling a rocket's acceleration

B. What feelings and sensations do you think Hadfield is trying to convey with these descriptions? Choose words below that apply to each description, or use your own. Discuss your ideas with a partner.

| a sense of awe | admiration | astonishment | fascination |
| powerlessness | shock | terror | joy |

CRITICAL THINKING

Interpreting. Hadfield says that when you look down on the Earth, "if your jaw could drop, it would." What do you think he means? Discuss your ideas with a partner.

Earth as seen from space

PART 2

"I CAN'T SEE."

RECOGNIZING MAIN IDEAS

Watch (▶) the second part of the talk. What are the main ideas of this segment? Choose the best options to complete a summary of the main ideas.

1. Instead of feeling panic, Hadfield was able to respond calmly mainly because _____.

   a. he had practiced exactly the same situation before

   b. he was able to think rationally about his fear

   c. he was able to get help quickly

   d. he developed a new solution to the problem

2. As a result of his experience of going blind, he realized that _____.

   a. all our fears are irrational

   b. we can learn to control our fear

   c. fear is normally beyond our control

   d. fear stops us from making progress

UNDERSTANDING A SEQUENCE OF EVENTS

A. Hadfield describes how he went blind in space. Number the events in the order they happened.

   _____ He continued working.

   _3_ He didn't know what to do next.

   _____ He was completely blind.

   _1_ He was on a spacewalk.

   _____ He managed to get back to the spacecraft.

   _____ His crewmate wiped his eyes.

   _____ His left eye closed with pain.

   _9_ He realized what had gotten into his eye.

   _____ Some liquid moved across into his right eye.

B. Which of the following factors helped Hadfield to deal with this situation? Check (✔) the ones he mentions.

   ☐ a. He had clear instructions from mission control on what to do next.

   ☐ b. He was still able to hear and talk.

   ☐ c. He had been underwater thousands of times.

   ☐ d. He knew he could find a way back.

   ☐ e. He knew that the tears would eventually dilute the liquid.

   ☐ f. He had experienced this situation before.

   ☐ g. There was another astronaut who could help.

   ☐ h. They had practiced crew rescue techniques.

EXPLORE MORE

Learn more about Chris Hadfield's experiences by watching his full TED Talk at TED.com. How did his experience in space help him change his attitude toward life? Share your information with the class.

Project

Finalist Jock Elliot (left) waits nervously as he prepares to give a presentation at the International World Championship of Public Speaking in Las Vegas.

A. **Work in a group of three. You are going to design a three-day training course for people who have one of the following fears.**

- Fear of public speaking
- Fear of heights
- Fear of flying
- Fear of elevators
- Fear of germs

In your group:

- brainstorm ideas for activities to include in your course.
- consider possible problems and drawbacks.
- describe what your goals and activities are for each day.
- draw a fear ladder on a poster or use presentation slides to illustrate your course.

B. **Present your plan to the class.**

1. Assign a part to each member of your group. Remember to introduce your training course and explain what its aims are and who it is for.

2. Make sure each member of the group has equal time to present their part.

3. Time your presentation so that you can finish it within your time limit. Make your presentation engaging and brief, but with sufficient detail so that your audience will understand your ideas.

EXPLORE MORE

Find out about how people can overcome another common fear at: natgeotv.com/uk/air-crash-investigation/fear-of-flying. Share what you learn with your class.

TEDTALK VIDEO TRANSCRIPTS

LOUIE SCHWARTZBERG

Hidden Miracles of the Natural World

Part 1

What is the intersection between technology, art, and science? Curiosity and wonder, because it drives us to explore, because we're surrounded by things we can't see. And I love to use film to take us on a journey through portals of time and space, to make the invisible visible, because what that does, it expands our horizons, it transforms our perception, it opens our minds and it touches our heart. So here are some scenes from my 3D IMAX film, "Mysteries of the Unseen World."

There is movement which is too slow for our eyes to detect, and time-lapse makes us discover and broaden our perspective of life. We can see how organisms emerge and grow, how a vine survives by creeping from the forest floor to look at the sunlight. And at the grand scale, time-lapse allows us to see our planet in motion. We can view not only the vast sweep of nature, but the restless movement of humanity. Each streaking dot represents a passenger plane, and by turning air traffic data into time-lapse imagery, we can see something that's above us constantly but invisible: the vast network of air travel over the United States. We can do the same thing with ships at sea. We can turn data into a time-lapse view of a global economy in motion. And decades of data give us the view of our entire planet as a single organism sustained by currents circulating throughout the oceans and by clouds swirling through the atmosphere, pulsing with lightning, crowned by the aurora borealis. It may be the ultimate time-lapse image: the anatomy of Earth brought to life.

At the other extreme, there are things that move too fast for our eyes, but we have technology that can look into that world as well. With high-speed cameras, we can do the opposite of time-lapse. We can shoot images that are thousands of times faster than our vision. And we can see how nature's ingenious devices work, and perhaps we can even imitate them. When a dragonfly flutters by, you may not realize, but it's the greatest flier in nature. It can hover, fly backwards, even upside down. And by tracking markers on an insect's wings, we can visualize the air flow that they produce. Nobody knew the secret, but high-speed shows that a dragonfly can move all four wings in different directions at the same time. And what we learn can lead us to new kinds of robotic flyers that can expand our vision of important and remote places.

Part 2

We're giants, and we're unaware of things that are too small for us to see. The electron microscope fires electrons which creates images which can magnify things by as much as a million times. This is the egg of a butterfly. And there are unseen creatures living all over your body, including mites that spend their entire lives dwelling on your eyelashes, crawling over your skin at night. Can you guess what this is? Shark skin. A caterpillar's mouth. The eye of a fruit fly. An eggshell. A flea. A snail's tongue. We think we know most of the animal kingdom, but there may be millions of tiny species waiting to be discovered.

A spider also has great secrets, because spider's silk thread is pound for pound stronger than steel but completely elastic. This journey will take us all the way down to the nano world. The silk is 100 times thinner than human hair. On there is bacteria, and near that bacteria, 10 times smaller, a virus. Inside of that, 10 times smaller, three strands of DNA, and nearing the limit of our most powerful microscopes, single carbon atoms.

With the tip of a powerful microscope, we can actually move atoms and begin to create amazing nano devices. Some could one day patrol our body for all kinds of diseases and clean out clogged arteries along the way. Tiny chemical machines of the future can one day, perhaps, repair DNA. We are on the threshold of extraordinary advances, born of our drive to unveil the mysteries of life.

So under an endless rain of cosmic dust, the air is full of pollen, micro-diamonds, and jewels from other planets, and supernova explosions. People go about their lives surrounded by the unseeable. Knowing that there's so much around us we can see forever changes our understanding of the world, and by looking at unseen worlds, we recognize that we exist in the living universe, and this new perspective creates wonder and inspires us to become explorers in our own backyards.

Who knows what awaits to be seen and what new wonders will transform our lives?

We'll just have to see.

Thank you.

ARIANNA HUFFINGTON
How to Succeed? Get More Sleep

Part 1

My big idea is a very, very small idea that can unlock billions of big ideas that are at the moment dormant inside us. And my little idea that will do that is sleep.

This is a room of type-A women. This is a room of sleep-deprived women. And I learned the hard way, the value of sleep. Two-and-a-half years ago, I fainted from exhaustion. I hit my head on my desk. I broke my cheekbone. I got five stitches on my right eye. And I began the journey of rediscovering the value of sleep. And in the course of that, I studied, I met with medical doctors, scientists, and I'm here to tell you that the way to a more productive, more inspired, more joyful life is getting enough sleep.

Part 2

And we women are going to lead the way in this new revolution, this new feminist issue. We are literally going to sleep our way to the top, literally.

Because unfortunately for men, sleep deprivation has become a virility symbol. I was recently having dinner with a guy who bragged that he had only gotten four hours' sleep the night before. And I felt like saying to him—but I didn't say it—I felt like saying, "You know what? If you had gotten five, this dinner would have been a lot more interesting."

There is now a kind of sleep deprivation one-upmanship. Especially here in Washington, if you try to make a breakfast date, and you say, "How about eight o'clock?" They're likely to tell you, "Eight o'clock is too late for me, but that's OK, you know, I can get a game of tennis in and do a few conference calls and meet you at eight." And they think that means that they are so incredibly busy and productive, but the truth is they're not, because we, at the moment, have had brilliant leaders in business, in finance, in politics, making terrible decisions. So a high I.Q. does not mean that you're a good leader, because the essence of leadership is being able to see the iceberg before it hits the *Titanic*. And we've had far too many icebergs hitting our *Titanics*.

In fact, I have a feeling that if Lehman Brothers was Lehman Brothers and Sisters, they might still be around. While all the brothers were busy just being hyper-connected 24/7, maybe a sister would have noticed the iceberg, because she would have woken up from a seven-and-a-half- or eight-hour sleep and have been able to see the big picture.

So as we are facing all the multiple crises in our world at the moment, what is good for us on a personal level, what's going to bring more joy, gratitude, effectiveness in our lives and be the best for our own careers is also what is best for the world. So I urge you to shut your eyes and discover the great ideas that lie inside us, to shut your engines and discover the power of sleep.

Thank you.

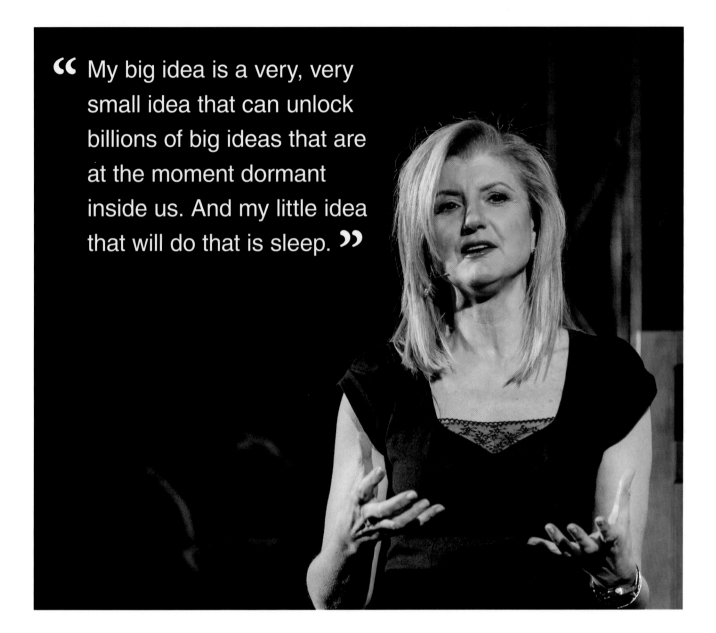

" My big idea is a very, very small idea that can unlock billions of big ideas that are at the moment dormant inside us. And my little idea that will do that is sleep. "

NEIL HARBISSON
I Listen to Color

Part 1

Well, I was born with a rare visual condition called achromatopsia, which is total color blindness, so I've never seen color, and I don't know what color looks like, because I come from a grayscale world. To me, the sky is always gray, flowers are always gray, and television is still in black and white.

But, since the age of 21, instead of seeing color, I can hear color. In 2003, I started a project with computer scientist Adam Montandon, and the result, with further collaborations with Peter Kese from Slovenia and Matias Lizana from Barcelona, is this electronic eye. It's a color sensor that detects the color frequency in front of me—and sends this frequency to a chip installed at the back of my head, and I hear the color in front of me through the bone, through bone conduction. So, for example, if I have, like—this is the sound of purple. For example, this is the sound of grass. This is red, like TED. This is the sound of a dirty sock. Which is like yellow, this one.

So I've been hearing color all the time for eight years, since 2004, so I find it completely normal now to hear color all the time. At the start, though, I had to memorize the names you give for each color, so I had to memorize the notes, but after some time, all this information became a perception. I didn't have to think about the notes. And after some time, this perception became a feeling. I started to have favorite colors, and I started to dream in colors.

So, when I started to dream in color is when I felt that the software and my brain had united, because in my dreams, it was my brain creating electronic sounds. It wasn't the software, so that's when I started to feel like a cyborg. It's when I started to feel that the cybernetic device was no longer a device. It had become a part of my body, an extension of my senses, and after some time, it even became a part of my official image.

This is my passport from 2004. You're not allowed to appear on U.K. passports with electronic equipment, but I insisted to the passport office that what they were seeing was actually a new part of my body, an extension of my brain, and they finally accepted me to appear with the passport photo. . . .

Part 2

So I really enjoy creating, like, sound portraits of people. Instead of drawing someone's face, like drawing the shape, I point at them with the eye and I write down the different notes I hear, and then I create sound portraits. Here's some faces.

Yeah, Nicole Kidman sounds good. Some people, I would never relate, but they sound similar. Prince Charles has some similarities with Nicole Kidman. They have similar sound of eyes. So you relate people that you wouldn't relate, and you can actually also create concerts by looking at the audience faces. So I connect the eye, and then I play the audience's faces. The good thing about this is, if the concert doesn't sound good, it's their fault. It's not my fault, because . . .

And so another thing that happens is that I started having this secondary effect that normal sounds started to become color. I heard a telephone tone, and it felt green because it sounded just like the color green. The BBC beeps, they sound turquoise, and listening to Mozart became a yellow experience, so I started to paint music and paint people's voices, because people's voices have frequencies that I relate to color.

And here's some music translated into color. For example, Mozart, "Queen of the Night," looks like this. Very yellow and very colorful, because there's many different frequencies. And this is a completely different song. It's Justin Bieber's "Baby." It is very pink and very yellow. . . .

So I got to a point when I was able to perceive 360 colors, just like human vision. I was able to differentiate all the degrees of the color wheel. But then, I just thought that this human vision wasn't good enough. There's many, many more colors around us that we cannot perceive, but that electronic eyes can perceive. So I decided to continue extending my color senses, and I added infrared and I added ultraviolet to the color-to-sound scale, so now I can hear colors that the human eye cannot perceive. . . .

We should all think that knowledge comes from our senses, so if we extend our senses, we will consequently extend our knowledge. I think life will be much more exciting when we stop creating applications for mobile phones and we start creating applications for our own body. I think this will be a big, big change that we'll see during this century.

So I do encourage you all to think about which senses you'd like to extend. I would encourage you to become a cyborg. You won't be alone. Thank you.

This is an edited version of Harbisson's 2012 TED Talk. To watch the full talk, visit TED.com

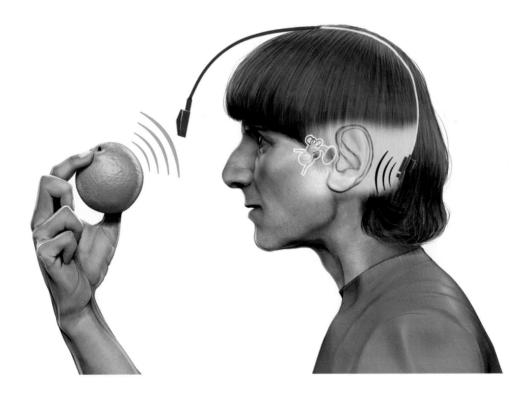

NIC MARKS
The Happy Planet Index

Part 1

And really, this is what I've done with my adult life—is think about how do we measure happiness, how do we measure well-being, how can we do that within environmental limits. And we created, at the organization I work for, the New Economics Foundation, something we call the Happy Planet Index, because we think people should be happy and the planet should be happy. Why don't we create a measure of progress that shows that? And what we do, is we say that the ultimate outcome of a nation is how successful is it at creating happy and healthy lives for its citizens. That should be the goal of every nation on the planet. But we have to remember that there's a fundamental input to that, and that is how many of the planet's resources we use. We all have one planet. We all have to share it. It is the ultimate scarce resource, the one planet that we share. And economics is very interested in scarcity. When it has a scarce resource that it wants to turn into a desirable outcome, it thinks in terms of efficiency. It thinks in terms of how much bang do we get for our buck. And this is a measure of how much well-being we get for our planetary resource use. It is an efficiency measure. And probably the easiest way to show you that, is to show you this graph.

Running horizontally along the graph, is "Ecological footprint," which is a measure of how much resources we use and how much pressure we put on the planet. More is bad. Running vertically upwards, is a measure called "Happy life years." It's about the well-being of nations. It's like a happiness adjusted life-expectancy. It's like quality and quantity of life in nations. And the yellow dot there you see, is the global average. Now, there's a huge array of nations around that global average. To the top right of the graph, are countries which are doing reasonably well and producing well-being, but they're using a lot of planet to get there. They are the U.S.A., other Western countries going across in those triangles and a few Gulf states in there, actually. Conversely, at the bottom left of the graph, are countries that are not producing much well-being —typically, sub-Saharan Africa. In Hobbesian terms, life is short and brutish there. Average life expectancy in many of these countries is only 40 years. Malaria, HIV/AIDS are killing a lot of people in these regions of the world.

But now for the good news! There are some countries up there, yellow triangles, that are doing better than global average, that are heading up towards the top left of the graph.

This is an aspirational graph. We want to be top left, where good lives don't cost the earth. They're Latin American. The country on its own up at the top is a place I haven't been to. Maybe some of you have: Costa Rica. Costa Rica—average life expectancy is 78-and-a-half years. That is longer than in the U.S.A. They are, according to the latest Gallup world poll, the happiest nation on the planet—than anybody; more than Switzerland and Denmark. They are the happiest place. They are doing that on a quarter of the resources that are used typically in [the] Western world—a quarter of the resources.

What's going on there? What's happening in Costa Rica? We can look at some of the data. 99 percent of their electricity comes from renewable resources. Their government is one of the first to commit to be carbon neutral by 2021. They abolished the army in 1949—1949. And they invested in social programs—health and education. They have one of the highest literacy rates in Latin America and in the world. And they have that Latin vibe, don't they? They have the social connectedness. The challenge is, that possibly—and the thing we might have to think about—is that the future might not be North American, might not be Western European. It might be Latin American. And the challenge, really, is to pull the global average up here. That's what we need to do. And if we're going to do that, we need to pull countries from the bottom, and we need to pull countries from the right of the graph. And then we're starting to create a happy planet. That's one way of looking at it. . . .

Why is it, on the radio news every evening, I hear the FTSE 100, the Dow Jones, the dollar-pound ratio—I don't even know which way the dollar-pound should go to be good news. And why do I hear that? Why don't I hear how much energy Britain used yesterday, or America used yesterday? Did we meet our three percent annual target on reducing carbon emissions? That's how you create a collective goal. You put it out there into the media and start thinking about it. And we need positive feedback loops for increasing well-being. At a government level, they might create national accounts of well-being. At a business level, you might look at the well-being of your employees, which we know is really linked to creativity, which is linked to innovation, and we're going to need a lot of innovation to deal with those environmental issues. At a personal level, we need these nudges too. . . .

Part 2

What are the five things that you should do every day to be happier?

We did a project for the Government Office of Science a couple of years ago, a big program called the Foresight program—lots and lots of people—involved lots of experts—everything evidence based—a huge tome. But a piece of work we did was on: What five positive actions can you do to improve well-being in your life? And the point of these is they are, not quite, the secrets of happiness, but they are things that I think happiness will flow out the side from.

And the first of these is to connect, is that your social relationships are the most important cornerstones of your life. Do you invest the time with your loved ones that you could do, and energy? Keep building them. The second one is be active. Fastest way out of a bad mood: Step outside, go for a walk, turn the radio on and dance. Being active is great for our positive mood. The third one is take notice. How aware are you of things going on around the world, the seasons changing, people around you? Do you notice what's bubbling up for you and trying to emerge? Based on a lot of evidence for mindfulness, cognitive behavioral therapy, very strong for our well-being. The fourth is keep learning and keep is important—learning throughout the whole life course. Older people who keep learning and are curious, they have much better health outcomes than those who start to close down. But it doesn't have to be formal learning; it's not knowledge based. It's more curiosity. It can be learning to cook a new dish, picking up an instrument you forgot as a child. Keep learning. And the final one is that most anti-economic of activities, but give. Our generosity, our altruism, our compassion, are all hardwired to the reward mechanism in our brain. We feel good if we give. You can do an experiment where you give two groups of people a hundred dollars in the morning. You tell one of them to spend it on themselves and one on other people. You measure their happiness at the end of the day, that those that have gone and spent on other people are much happier that those that spent it on themselves.

And these five ways, which we put onto these handy postcards, I would say, don't have to cost the Earth. They don't have any carbon content. They don't need a lot of material goods to be satisfied. And so I think it's really quite feasible that happiness does not cost the Earth. . . .

This is an edited version of Marks's 2010 TED Talk.
To watch the full talk, visit TED.com

STEFAN SAGMEISTER

The Power of Time Off

Part 1

I run a design studio in New York. Every seven years, I close it for one year to pursue some little experiments, things that are always difficult to accomplish during the regular working year. In that year, we are not available for any of our clients. We are totally closed. And as you can imagine, it is a lovely and very energetic time.

I originally had opened the studio in New York to combine my two loves, music and design. And we created videos and packaging for many musicians that you know, and for even more that you've never heard of. As I realized, just like with many, many things in my life that I actually love, I adapt to it. And I get, over time, bored by them. And for sure, in our case, our work started to look the same. You see here a glass eye in a die cut of a book. Quite the similar idea, then, a perfume packaged in a book, in a die cut. So I decided to close it down for one year.

Also is the knowledge that right now we spend about in the first 25 years of our lives learning, then there is another 40 years that's really reserved for working. And then tacked on at the end of it are about 15 years for retirement. And I thought it might be helpful to basically cut off five of those retirement years and intersperse them in between those working years. That's clearly enjoyable for myself. But probably even more important is that the work that comes out of these years flows back into the company and into society at large, rather than just benefiting a grandchild or two.

There is a fellow TEDster who spoke two years ago, Jonathan Haidt, who defined his work into three different levels. And they rang very true for me. I can see my work as a job. I do it for money. I likely already look forward to the weekend on Thursdays. And I probably will need a hobby as a leveling mechanism. In a career I'm definitely more engaged. But at the same time, there will be periods when I think is all that really hard work really worth my while? While in the third one, in the calling, very much likely I would do it also if I wouldn't be financially compensated for it. . . .

Part 2

If I look at my cycle, seven years, one-year sabbatical, it's 12.5 percent of my time. And if I look at companies that are actually more successful than mine, 3M since the 1930s is giving all their engineers 15 percent to pursue whatever they want. There [are] some good successes. Scotch tape came out of this program, as well as Art Fry developed sticky notes from during his personal time for 3M. Google, of course, very famously gives 20 percent for their software engineers to pursue their own personal projects. . . .

When I had the idea of doing one, the process was I made the decision and I put it into my daily planner book. And then I told as many, many people as I possibly could about it so that there was no way that I could chicken out later on.

In the beginning, on the first sabbatical, it was rather disastrous. I had thought that I should do this without any plan, that this vacuum of time somehow would be wonderful and enticing for idea generation. It was not. I just, without a plan, I just reacted to little requests, not work requests—those I all said no to—but other little requests. Sending mail to Japanese design magazines and things like that. So I became my own intern.

And I very quickly made a list of the things that I was interested in, put them in a hierarchy, divided them into chunks of time and then made a plan, very much like in grade school. What does it say here? Monday, 8 to 9: story writing; 9 to 10: future thinking. Was not very successful. And so on and so forth. And that actually, specifically as a starting point of the first sabbatical, worked really well for me. What came out of it? I really got close to design again. I had fun. Financially, seen over the long term, it was actually successful. Because of the improved quality, we could ask for higher prices.

And probably most importantly, basically everything we've done in the seven years following the first sabbatical came out of thinking of that one single year.

And I'll show you a couple of projects that came out of the seven years following that sabbatical. . . .

This is a whole wall of bananas at different ripenesses on the opening day in this gallery in New York. It says, "Self-confidence produces fine results." This is after a week. After two weeks, three weeks, four weeks, five weeks. And you see the self-confidence almost comes back, but not quite. These are some pictures visitors sent to me.

And then the city of Amsterdam gave us a plaza and asked us to do something. We used the stone plates as a grid for our little piece. We got 250,000 coins from the central bank, at different darknesses. So we got brand-new ones, shiny ones, medium ones, and very old, dark ones. And with the help of 100 volunteers, over a week, created this fairly floral typography that spelled, "Obsessions make my life worse and my work better." . . .

We are also working on the start of a bigger project in Bali. It's a movie about happiness. And here we asked some nearby pigs to do the titles for us. They weren't quite slick enough. So we asked the goose to do it again, and hoped she would do somehow, a more elegant or pretty job. And I think she overdid it. Just a bit too ornamental. And my studio

is very close to the monkey forest. And the monkeys in that monkey forest looked, actually, fairly happy. So we asked those guys to do it again. They did a fine job, but had a couple of readability problems. So of course whatever you don't really do yourself doesn't really get done properly. That film we'll be working on for the next two years. . . .

Thank you.

This is an edited version of Sagmeister's 2009 TED Talk. To watch the full talk, visit TED.com

JOHN McWHORTER

Txtng Is Killing Language. JK!!!

Part 1

What texting is, despite the fact that it involves the brute mechanics of something that we call writing, is fingered speech. That's what texting is. Now we can write the way we talk. And it's a very interesting thing, but nevertheless, easy to think that still it represents some sort of decline. We see this general bagginess of the structure, the lack of concern with rules and the way that we're used to learning on the blackboard, and so we think that something has gone wrong. It's a very natural sense.

But the fact of the matter is that what is going on is a kind of emergent complexity. That's what we're seeing in this fingered speech. And in order to understand it, what we want to see is the way, in this new kind of language, there is new structure coming up.

And so, for example, there is in texting a convention, which is LOL. Now LOL, we generally think of as meaning "laughing out loud." And of course, theoretically, it does, and if you look at older texts, then people used it to actually indicate laughing out loud. But if you text now, or if you are someone who is aware of the substrate of texting the way it's become, you'll notice that LOL does not mean laughing out loud anymore. It's evolved into something that is much subtler.

This is an actual text that was done by a non-male person of about 20 years old not too long ago.

"I love the font you're using, btw."

Julie: "lol thanks gmail is being slow right now"

Now if you think about it, that's not funny. No one's laughing. And yet, there it is, so you assume there's been some kind of hiccup.

Then Susan says "lol, I know," again more guffawing than we're used to when you're talking about these inconveniences.

So Julie says, "I just sent you an email."

Susan: "lol, I see it."

Very funny people, if that's what LOL means.

This Julie says, "So what's up?"

Susan: "lol, I have to write a 10 page paper."

She's not amused. Let's think about it. LOL is being used in a very particular way. It's a marker of empathy. It's a marker of accommodation. We linguists call things like that pragmatic particles. Any spoken language that's used by real people has them. If you happen to speak Japanese, think about that little word *ne* that you use at the end of a lot of sentences. If you listen to the way black youth today speak, think about the use of the word *yo*. Whole dissertations could be written about it, and probably are being written about it. A pragmatic particle, that's what LOL has gradually become. It's a way of using the language between actual people. . . .

Part 2

Another example is "slash." Now, we can use *slash* in the way that we're used to, along the lines of, "We're going to have a party-slash-networking session." That's kind of like what we're at. *Slash* is used in a very different way in texting among young people today. It's used to change the scene.

So for example, this Sally person says, "So I need to find people to chill with" and Jake says, "Haha"—you could write a dissertation about "Haha" too, but we don't have time for that—"Haha so you're going by yourself? Why?"

Sally: "For this summer program at NYU."

Jake: "Haha. Slash I'm watching this video with suns players trying to shoot with one eye."

The slash is interesting. I don't really even know what Jake is talking about after that, but you notice that he's changing the topic. Now that seems kind of mundane, but think about how in real life, if we're having a conversation and we want to change the topic, there are ways of doing it gracefully. You don't just zip right into it. You'll pat your thighs and look wistfully off into the distance, or you'll say something like, "Hmm, makes you think"—when it really didn't, but what you're really—what you're really trying to do is change the topic. You can't do that while you're texting, and so ways are developing of doing it within this medium. All spoken languages have what a linguist calls a new information marker—or two, or three. Texting has developed one from this slash. . . .

And so, the way I'm thinking of texting these days is that what we're seeing is a whole new way of writing that young people are developing, which they're using alongside their ordinary writing skills, and that means that they're able to do two things. Increasing evidence is that being bilingual is cognitively beneficial. That's also true of being bidialectal. That's certainly true of being bidialectal in terms of your writing. And so texting actually is evidence of a balancing act that young people are using today, not consciously, of course, but it's an expansion of their linguistic repertoire . . .

This is an edited version of McWhorter's 2013 TED Talk.
To watch the full talk, visit TED.com

CHIMAMANDA NGOZI ADICHIE
The Danger of a Single Story

Part 1

I'm a storyteller. And I would like to tell you a few personal stories about what I like to call "the danger of the single story." I grew up on a university campus in eastern Nigeria. My mother says that I started reading at the age of two, although I think four is probably close to the truth. So I was an early reader, and what I read were British and American children's books.

I was also an early writer, and when I began to write, at about the age of seven, stories in pencil with crayon illustrations that my poor mother was obligated to read, I wrote exactly the kinds of stories I was reading: All my characters were white and blue-eyed, they played in the snow, they ate apples, and they talked a lot about the weather, how lovely it was that the sun had come out. Now, this despite the fact that I lived in Nigeria. I had never been outside Nigeria. We didn't have snow, we ate mangoes, and we never talked about the weather, because there was no need to.

My characters also drank a lot of ginger beer because the characters in the British books I read drank ginger beer. Never mind that I had no idea what ginger beer was. And for many years afterwards, I would have a desperate desire to taste ginger beer. But that is another story.

What this demonstrates, I think, is how impressionable and vulnerable we are in the face of a story, particularly as children. Because all I had read were books in which characters were foreign, I had become convinced that books by their very nature had to have foreigners in them and had to be about things with which I could not personally identify. Now, things changed when I discovered African books. There weren't many of them available, and they weren't quite as easy to find as the foreign books.

But because of writers like Chinua Achebe and Camara Laye, I went through a mental shift in my perception of literature. I realized that people like me, girls with skin the color of chocolate, whose kinky hair could not form ponytails, could also exist in literature. I started to write about things I recognized.

Now, I loved those American and British books I read. They stirred my imagination. They opened up new worlds for me. But the unintended consequence was that I did not know that people like me could exist in literature. So what the discovery of African writers did for me was this: It saved me from having a single story of what books are.

Part 2

I come from a conventional, middle-class Nigerian family. My father was a professor. My mother was an administrator. And so we had, as was the norm, live-in domestic help, who would often come from nearby rural villages. So the year I turned eight, we got a new house boy. His name was Fide. The only thing my mother told us about him was that his family was very poor. My mother sent yams and rice, and our old clothes, to his family. And when I didn't finish my dinner my mother would say, "Finish your food! Don't you know? People like Fide's family have nothing." So I felt enormous pity for Fide's family.

Then one Saturday we went to his village to visit, and his mother showed us a beautifully patterned basket made of dyed raffia that his brother had made. I was startled. It had not occurred to me that anybody in his family could actually make something. All I had heard about them was how poor they were, so that it had become impossible for me to see them as anything else but poor. Their poverty was my single story of them.

Years later, I thought about this when I left Nigeria to go to university in the United States. I was 19. My American roommate was shocked by me. She asked where I had learned to speak English so well, and was confused when I said that Nigeria happened to have English as its official language. She asked if she could listen to what she called my "tribal music," and was consequently very disappointed when I produced my tape of Mariah Carey. She assumed that I did not know how to use a stove.

What struck me was this: She had felt sorry for me even before she saw me. Her default position toward me, as an African, was a kind of patronizing, well-meaning pity. My roommate had a single story of Africa: a single story of catastrophe. In this single story, there was no possibility of Africans being similar to her in any way, no possibility of feelings more complex than pity, no possibility of a connection as human equals. . . .

But I must quickly add that I, too, am just as guilty in the question of the single story. A few years ago, I visited Mexico from the U.S. The political climate in the U.S. at the time was tense, and there were debates going on about immigration. And, as often happens in America, immigration became synonymous with Mexicans. There were endless stories of Mexicans as people who were fleecing the healthcare system, sneaking across the border, being arrested at the border, that sort of thing.

I remember walking around on my first day in Guadalajara, watching the people going to work, rolling up tortillas in the marketplace, smoking, laughing. I remember first feeling slight surprise. And then I was overwhelmed with shame. I realized that I had been so immersed in the media coverage of Mexicans that they had become one thing in my mind: the abject immigrant. I had bought into the single story of Mexicans, and I could not have been more ashamed of myself. So that is how to create a single story, show a people as one thing, as only one thing, over and over again, and that is what they become.

. . . But to insist on only these negative stories is to flatten my experience and to overlook the many other stories that formed me. The single story creates stereotypes, and the problem with stereotypes is not that they are untrue, but that they are incomplete. They make one story become the only story. . . .

I've always felt that it is impossible to engage properly with a place or a person without engaging with all of the stories of that place and that person. The consequence of the single story is this: It robs people of dignity. It makes our recognition of our equal humanity difficult. It emphasizes how we are different rather than how we are similar.

. . . I teach writing workshops in Lagos every summer, and it is amazing to me how many people apply, how many people are eager to write, to tell stories.

My Nigerian publisher and I have just started a non-profit called Farafina Trust, and we have big dreams of building libraries and refurbishing libraries that already exist and providing books for state schools that don't have anything in their libraries, and also of organizing lots and lots of workshops, in reading and writing, for all the people who are eager to tell our many stories. Stories matter. Many stories matter. Stories have been used to dispossess and to malign, but stories can also be used to empower and to humanize. Stories can break the dignity of a people, but stories can also repair that broken dignity. . . .

This is an edited version of Adichie's 2009 TED Talk.
To watch the full talk, visit TED.com

Unit 8

SUSAN CAIN

The Power of Introverts

Part 1

A third to a half of the population are introverts—a third to a half. So that's one out of every two or three people you know. So even if you're an extrovert yourself, I'm talking about your coworkers and your spouses and your children and the person sitting right next to you right now—all of them subject to this bias that is pretty deep and real in our society. We all internalize it from a very early age without even having a language for what we're doing. . . .

But now, here's where the bias comes in. Our most important institutions, our schools and our workplaces, they are designed mostly for extroverts and for extroverts' need for lots of stimulation. And also, we're living through this belief system, we have a belief system right now that I call the new groupthink, which holds that all creativity and all productivity comes from a very oddly gregarious place.

So if you picture the typical classroom nowadays: When I was going to school, we sat in rows. We sat in rows of desks like this, and we did most of our work pretty autonomously. But nowadays, your typical classroom has pods of desks—four or five or six or seven kids all facing each other. And kids are working in countless group assignments. Even in subjects like math and creative writing, which you would think would depend on solo flights of thought, kids are now expected to act as committee members. And for the kids who prefer to go off by themselves or just to work alone, those kids are seen as outliers often or, worse, as problem cases. And the vast majority of teachers reports believing that the ideal student is an extrovert as opposed to an introvert, even though introverts actually get better grades and are more knowledgeable, according to research.

OK, same thing is true in our workplaces. We now, most of us, work in open plan offices, without walls, where we are subject to the constant noise and gaze of our coworkers. And when it comes to leadership, introverts are routinely passed over for leadership positions, even though introverts tend to be very careful, much less likely to take outsized risks—which is something we might all favor nowadays. And interesting research by Adam Grant at the Wharton School has found that introverted leaders often deliver better outcomes than extroverts do, because when they are managing proactive employees, they're much more likely to let those employees run with their ideas, whereas an extrovert can, quite unwittingly, get so excited about things that they're putting their own stamp on things, and other people's ideas might not as easily then bubble up to the surface. . . .

Part 2

Now if all this is true, then why are we getting it so wrong? Why are we setting up our schools this way and our workplaces? And why are we making these introverts feel so guilty about wanting to just go off by themselves some of the time? One answer lies deep in our cultural history. Western societies, and in particular the U.S., have always favored the man of action over the man of contemplation and "man" of contemplation. But in America's early days, we lived in what historians call a culture of character, where we still, at that point, valued people for their inner selves and their moral rectitude. And if you look at the self-help books from this era, they all had titles with things like "Character, the Grandest Thing in the World." And they featured role models like Abraham Lincoln who was praised for being modest and unassuming. Ralph Waldo Emerson called him "A man who does not offend by superiority."

But then we hit the 20th century and we entered a new culture that historians call the culture of personality. What happened is we had evolved from an agricultural economy to a world of big business. And so suddenly people are moving from small towns to the cities. And instead of working alongside people they've known all their lives, now they are having to prove themselves in a crowd of strangers. So, quite understandably, qualities like magnetism and charisma suddenly come to seem really important. And sure enough, the self-help books change to meet these new needs and they start to have names like "How to Win Friends and Influence People." And they feature as their role models really great salesmen. So that's the world we're living in today. That's our cultural inheritance.

Now none of this is to say that social skills are unimportant, and I'm also not calling for the abolishing of teamwork at all. The same religions who send their sages off to lonely mountain tops also teach us love and trust. And the problems that we are facing today in fields like science and in economics are so vast and so complex that we are going to need armies of people coming together to solve them working together. But I am saying that the more freedom that we give introverts to be themselves, the more likely that they are to come up with their own unique solutions to these problems. . . .

So I just published a book about introversion, and it took me about seven years to write. And for me, that seven years was like total bliss, because I was reading, I was writing, I was thinking, I was researching. It was my version of my grandfather's hours a day alone in his library. But now all of a sudden my job is very different, and my job is to be out here talking about it, talking about introversion. And that's a lot harder for me, because as honored as I am to be here with all of you right now, this is not my natural milieu.

So I prepared for moments like these as best I could. I spent the last year practicing public speaking every chance I could get. And I call this my "year of speaking dangerously." And that actually helped a lot. But I'll tell you, what helps even more is my sense, my belief, my hope that when it comes to our attitudes to introversion and to quiet and to solitude, we truly are poised on the brink of dramatic change. . .

So I wish you the best of all possible journeys and the courage to speak softly.

Thank you very much.

This is an edited version of Cain's 2012 TED Talk.
To watch the full talk, visit TED.com

SUSAN SAVAGE-RUMBAUGH
The Gentle Genius of Bonobos

Part 1

There are many people who think that the animal world is hard-wired and that there's something very, very special about man. Maybe it's his ability to have causal thought. Maybe it's something special in his brain that allows him to have language. Maybe it's something special in his brain that allows him to make tools or have mathematics . . .

So what I want to do now is introduce you to a species called the bonobo. This is Kanzi. He's a bonobo. Right now, he's in a forest in Georgia. His mother originally came from a forest in Africa. And she came to us when she was just at puberty, about six or seven years of age. . . .

This is Kanzi and I, in the forest. None of the things you will see in this particular video are trained. None of them are tricks. They all happened to be captured on film spontaneously, by NHK of Japan. We have eight bonobos.

Savage-Rumbaugh (video): Look at all this stuff that's here for our campfire.

S-R: An entire family at our research center.

S-R (video): You going to help get some sticks? Good. We need more sticks, too. I have a lighter in my pocket if you need one. That's a wasps' nest. You can get it out. I hope I have a lighter. You can use the lighter to start the fire.

S-R: So Kanzi is very interested in fire. He doesn't do it yet without a lighter, but I think if he saw someone do it, he might be able to do—make a fire without a lighter. He's learning about how to keep a fire going. He's learning the uses for a fire, just by watching what we do with fire.

. . . This is his sister. This is her first time to try to drive a golf cart.

S-R (video): Good-bye.

S-R: She's got the pedals down, but not the wheel. She switches from reverse to forward and she holds onto the wheel, rather than turns it.

Like us, she knows that that individual in the mirror is her.

Narrator: By raising bonobos in a culture that is both bonobo and human, and documenting their development across two decades, scientists are exploring how cultural forces may have operated during human evolution.

His name is Nyota. It means "star" in Swahili.

Panbanisha is trying to give Nyota a haircut with a pair of scissors. In the wild, the parent bonobo is known to groom its offspring. Here Panbanisha uses scissors, instead of her hands, to groom Nyota. Very impressive. Subtle maneuvering of the hands is required to perform delicate tasks like this. Nyota tries to imitate Panbanisha by using the scissors himself. Realizing that Nyota might get hurt, Panbanisha, like any human mother, carefully tugs to get the scissors back. . . .

He can now cut through tough animal hide.

S-R Kanzi's learned to make stone tools.

Narr: Kanzi now makes his tools, just as our ancestors may have made them, two-and-a-half million years ago—by holding the rocks in both hands, to strike one against the other. He has learned that by using both hands and aiming his glancing blows, he can make much larger, sharper flakes. Kanzi chooses a flake he thinks is sharp enough. The tough hide is difficult to cut, even with a knife. The rock that Kanzi is using is extremely hard and ideal for stone tool making, but difficult to handle, requiring great skill. Kanzi's rock is from Gona, Ethiopia, and is identical to that used by our African ancestors two-and-a-half million years ago. These are the rocks Kanzi used and these are the flakes he made. The flat sharp edges are like knife blades. Compare them to the tools our ancestors used; they bear a striking resemblance to Kanzi's.

Part 2

S-R: These are her symbols on her keyboard.

They speak when she touches them.

Narr: Panbanisha is communicating to Dr. Sue where she wants to go. "A-frame" represents a hut in the woods. Compare the chalk writing with the lexigram on the keyboard. Panbanisha began writing the lexigrams on the forest floor.

S-R (video): Very nice. Beautiful, Panbanisha.

S-R: At first we didn't really realize what she was doing, until we stood back and looked at it and rotated it.

Narr: This lexigram also refers to a place in the woods. The curved line is very similar to the lexigram. The next symbol Panbanisha writes represents "collar." It indicates the collar Panbanisha must wear when she goes out.

S-R: That's an institutional requirement.

Narr: This symbol is not as clear as the others, but one can see Panbanisha is trying to produce a curved line and several straight lines. Researchers began to record what Panbanisha said, by writing lexigrams on the floor with chalk. Panbanisha watched. Soon she began to write as well. The bonobo's abilities have stunned scientists around the world. How did they develop?

S-R (video): We found that the most important thing for permitting bonobos to acquire language is not to teach them. It's simply to use language around them, because the driving force in language acquisition is to understand what others, that are important to you, are saying to you. Once you have that capacity, the ability to produce language comes rather naturally and rather freely. So we want to create an environment in which bonobos, like all of the individuals with whom they are interacting—we want to create an environment in which they have fun, and an environment in which the others are meaningful individuals for them.

Narr: This environment brings out unexpected potential in Kanzi and Panbanisha. . . .

Researcher (video): OK, now get the monsters. Get them. Take the cherries, too. Now watch out, stay away from them now. Now you can chase them again. Time to chase them. Now you have to stay away. Get away. Run away. Run. Now we can chase them again. Go get them. Oh, no! Good, Kanzi. Very good. Thank you so much. . . .

S-R: So we have a bi-species environment; we call it a "panhomoculture." We're learning how to become like them. We're learning how to communicate with them, in really high-pitched tones. We're learning that they probably have a language in the wild. And they're learning to become like us. Because we believe that it's not biology; it's culture. So we're sharing tools and technology and language with another species.

Thank you.

This is an edited version of Savage-Rumbaugh's 2004 TED Talk. To watch the full talk, visit TED.com

CHRIS HADFIELD
What I Learned from Going Blind in Space

Part 1

What's the scariest thing you've ever done? Or another way to say it is, what's the most dangerous thing that you've ever done? And why did you do it? I know what the most dangerous thing is that I've ever done because NASA does the math. You look back to the first five shuttle launches, the odds of a catastrophic event during the first five shuttle launches was one in nine. And even when I first flew in the shuttle back in 1995, 74 shuttle flight, the odds were still now that we look back about one in 38 or so—one in 35, one in 40. Not great odds, so it's a really interesting day when you wake up at the Kennedy Space Center and you're going to go to space that day because you realize by the end of the day you're either going to be floating effortlessly, gloriously in space, or you'll be dead. . . .

Announcer: 12, 11, 10, nine, eight, seven, six—start, two, one, booster ignition, and liftoff of the space shuttle Discovery, returning to the space station, paving the way . . .

Hadfield: It is incredibly powerful to be on board one of these things. You are in the grip of something that is vastly more powerful than yourself. It's shaking you so hard you can't focus on the instruments in front of you. It's like you're in the jaws of some enormous dog and there's a foot in the small of your back pushing you into space, accelerating wildly straight up, shouldering your way through the air, and you're in a very complex place—paying attention, watching the vehicle go through each one of its wickets with a steadily increasing smile on your face. After two minutes, those solid rockets explode off and then you just have the liquid engines, the hydrogen and oxygen, and it's as if you're in a dragster with your foot to the floor and accelerating like you've never accelerated. You get lighter and lighter, the force gets on us heavier and heavier. It feels like someone's pouring cement on you or something. Until finally, after about eight minutes and 40 seconds or so, we are finally at exactly the right altitude, exactly the right speed, the right direction, the engine shut off, and we're weightless. And we're alive.

It's an amazing experience. But why would we take that risk? Why would you do something that dangerous?

In my case, the answer is fairly straightforward. I was inspired as a youngster that this is what I wanted to do. I watched the first people walk on the moon and to me, it was just an obvious thing—I want to somehow turn myself into that. But the real question is, how do you deal with the danger of it and the fear that comes from it? How do you deal with fear versus danger?

And having the goal in mind, thinking about where it might lead, directed me to a life of looking at all of the small details to allow this to become possible, to be able to launch and go help build a space station where you are on board a million-pound creation that's going around the world at five miles a second, eight kilometers a second, around the world 16 times a day, with experiments on board that are teaching us what the substance of the universe is made of and running 200 experiments inside. But maybe even more importantly, allowing us to see the world in a way that is impossible through any other means, to be able to look down and have—if your jaw could drop, it would—the jaw-dropping gorgeousness of the turning orb like a self-propelled art gallery of fantastic, constantly changing beauty that is the world itself. And you see, because of the speed, a sunrise or a sunset every 45 minutes for half a year.

And the most magnificent part of all that is to go outside on a spacewalk.

You are in a one-person spaceship that is your spacesuit, and you're going through space with the world. It's an entirely different perspective, you're not looking up at the universe, you and the Earth are going through the universe together. And you're holding on with one hand, looking at the world turn beside you. It's roaring silently with color and texture as it pours by just mesmerizingly next to you. And if you can tear your eyes away from that and you look under your arm down at the rest of everything, it's unfathomable blackness, with a texture you feel like you could stick your hand into. And you are holding on with one hand, one link to the other seven billion people.

Part 2

And I was outside on my first spacewalk when my left eye went blind, and I didn't know why. Suddenly my left eye slammed shut in great pain and I couldn't figure out why my eye wasn't working. I was thinking, what do I do next? I thought, well, maybe that's why we have two eyes, so I kept working. But unfortunately, without gravity, tears don't fall. So you just get a bigger and bigger ball of whatever that is mixed with your tears on your eye until eventually, the ball becomes so big that the surface tension takes it across the bridge of your nose like a tiny little waterfall and goes "goosh" into your other eye, and now I was completely blind outside the spaceship. . . .

If you're outside on a spacewalk and you're blinded, your natural reaction would be to panic, I think. It would make you nervous and worried. But we had considered all the venom, and we had practiced with a whole variety of different spider webs. We knew everything there is to know about the spacesuit and we trained underwater thousands of times. And we don't just practice things going right, we practice things going wrong all the time, so that you are constantly walking through those spider webs. And not just underwater, but also in virtual reality labs with the helmet and the gloves so you feel like it's realistic. So when you finally actually get outside on a spacewalk, it feels much different than it would if you just went out first time. And even if you're blinded, your natural, panicky reaction doesn't happen. Instead you kind of look around and go, "OK, I can't see, but I can hear, I can talk, Scott Parazynski is out here with me. He could come over and help me." We actually practiced incapacitated crew rescue, so he could float me like a blimp and stuff me into the airlock if he had to. I could find my own way back. It's not nearly as big a deal. And actually, if you keep on crying for a while, whatever that gunk was that's in your eye starts to

dilute and you can start to see again, and Houston, if you negotiate with them, they will let you then keep working. We finished everything on the spacewalk and when we came back inside, Jeff got some cotton batting and took the crusty stuff around my eyes, and it turned out it was just the anti-fog, sort of a mixture of oil and soap, that got in my eye. And now we use Johnson's No More Tears, which we probably should've been using right from the very beginning.

But the key to that is by looking at the difference between perceived danger and actual danger, where is the real risk? What is the real thing that you should be afraid of? Not just a generic fear of bad things happening. You can fundamentally change your reaction to things so that it allows you to go places and see things and do things that otherwise would be completely denied to you . . . where you can see the hardpan south of the Sahara, or you can see New York City in a way that is almost dreamlike, or the unconscious gingham of Eastern Europe fields or the Great Lakes as a collection of small puddles. You can see the fault lines of San Francisco and the way the water pours out under the bridge, just entirely different than any other way that you could have if you had not found a way to conquer your fear. You see a beauty that otherwise never would have happened. . . .

This is an edited version of Hadfield's 2014 TED Talk.
To watch the full talk, visit TED.com

VOCABULARY LOG

As you complete each unit, use this chart to record definitions and example sentences of key vocabulary. Add other useful words or phrases you learn.

Unit	Vocabulary	Definition/Example
1	attributed (to)*	
	challenge*	
	constant*	
	document*	
	illustrate*	
	issue*	
	primarily*	
	reinforce*	
	specifically*	
	transform*	
2	acknowledge*	
	apparently*	
	consequences*	
	crucial*	
	injury*	
	institute*	
	investigation*	
	legal*	
	medical*	
	ultimately*	
3	adapt*	
	advanced	
	component*	
	data*	
	implant	
	mechanical	
	networks*	
	permanently	
	remove*	
	utilize*	

Unit	Vocabulary	Definition/Example
4	aspiration	_____
	deconstruction	_____
	degradation	_____
	desolate	_____
	fundamental*	_____
	invest*	_____
	outcome*	_____
	promote*	_____
	civilization	_____
	worthwhile	_____
	_____	_____
5	couple*	_____
	enrich	_____
	ethics*	_____
	hesitate	_____
	income*	_____
	mentally*	_____
	physically*	_____
	pursue*	_____
	reliable*	_____
	reserve	_____
	_____	_____
6	conscious	_____
	decline*	_____
	edit*	_____
	expand (on)*	_____
	feedback	_____
	formal	_____
	linguist	_____
	logically*	_____
	mode*	_____
	spontaneous	_____
	_____	_____

* These words are on the Academic Word List (AWL), a list of the 570 most frequent word families in academic texts. The AWL does not include words that are among the most frequent 2,000 words of English. For more information, see www.victoria.ac.nz/lals/resources/academicwordlist/

Unit	Vocabulary	Definition/Example
7	apologize	
	attend	
	break out	
	break up	
	coincide*	
	diversity*	
	ignore*	
	isolated*	
	opponent	
	potential*	
8	colleague*	
	dominant	
	emphatically	
	insight*	
	instill	
	intuition	
	long (to be)	
	outgoing	
	psychologist*	
	solitude	
9	abstract*	
	adept (at)	
	capable*	
	contrary*	
	correspond to*	
	integrate*	
	intrigued (by)	
	remarkable	
	resonate	
	superior	

Unit	Vocabulary	Definition/Example
10	conduct*	
	countless	
	detach	
	emergency	
	exposure*	
	irrational	
	malfunction	
	overcome	
	stranded	
	unpredictable	
	_____	

Acknowledgements

The Authors and Publisher would like to thank the following teaching professionals for their valuable input during the development of this series:

Coleeta Paradise Abdullah, Certified Training Center; **Wilder Yesid Escobar Almeciga,** Universidad El Bosque; **Tara Amelia Arntsen,** Northern State University; **Mei-ho Chiu,** Soochow University; **Amy Cook,** Bowling Green State University; **Anthony Sean D'Amico,** SDH Institute; **Mariel Doyenart,** Alianza Cultural Uruguay-Estados Unidos; **Raichle Farrelly,** American University of Armenia; **Douglas E. Forster,** Japan Women's University; **Rosario Giraldez,** Alianza Cultural Uruguay Estados Unidos; **Floyd H. Graham III,** Kansai Gaidai University; **Jay Klaphake,** Kyoto University of Foreign Studies; **Anthony G. Lavigne,** Kansai Gaidai University; **Adriana Castañeda Londoño,** Centro Colombo Americano; **Alexandra Dylan Lowe,** SUNY Westchester Community College; **Elizabeth Ortiz Lozada,** COPEI–COPOL English Institute; **David Matijasevich,** Canadian Education College; **Jennie Popp,** Universidad Andrés Bello; **Ubon Pun-ubon,** Sripatum University; **Yoko Sakurai,** Aichi University; **Michael J. Sexton,** PSB Academy; **Jenay Seymour,** Hongik University; **Karenne Sylvester,** New College Manchester; **Mark S. Turnoy,** Chung-Ang University; **Hajime Uematsu,** Hirosaki University; **Nae-Dong Yang,** National Taiwan University;

And special thanks to: Aziz Abu Sarah, Winston Chen, Mary Kadera, Nic Marks, Louie Schwartzberg, FEI Institute, Shawn Rocco/Duke Medicine, New Economics Foundation and Lab42

Text Credits

10–13 Adapted from "Viewing Nature's Beauty Through a New Lens," by Sonia Harmon: NG Newswatch April 2014, **26–29** Adapted from "The Secrets of Sleep," by D. T. Max: NGM May 2010, **42–45** Adapted from "Behold, 6 real-life cyborgs," by Kate Torgovnick May: http://blog.ted.com July 20, 2012, **74–77** Adapted from "Leave work for a year to go live on a remote island? How a TED Talk inspired me to take a mid-career sabbatical," by Winston Chen: http://blog.ted.com July 8, 2014, **106–109** Adapted from "Why the World Cup is About More Than Soccer," by Aziz Abu Sarah: NG Newswatch July 2014, **138–141** Adapted from "The interspecies internet: Diana Reiss, Peter Gabriel, Neil Gershenfeld and Vint Cerf at TED2013," by Kate Torgovnick May: http://blog.ted.com February 28, 2013.

Photo and Infographic Credits

8–9 Christian Ziegler/National Geographic Creative; **10-11** University of Basel/National Geographic Studios; **12–13** University of Basel/National Geographic Studios; **14** (tr) University of Basel/National Geographic Studios; **16** (b) Jim Richardson/National Geographic Creative; **18–19** ©James Duncan Davidson/TED; **20** (br) Medford Taylor/National Geographic Creative; **22** (br) (bl) (cr) (cl) University of Basel/National Geographic Studios; **23** (t) Robert Clark/National Geographic Creative; **24–25** Xpacifica/National Geographic Creative; **26–27** Jianan Yu/Reuters; **28** Source: National Sleep Foundation; **29** (t) Mohamed Abd El Ghany/Reuters; **29** (bl) Jan-Peter Boening/Zenit/laif/Redux; **33** (br) Adnan Abidi/Reuters; **34–35** Michael Brands/TED; **39** (t) Maggie Steber/National Geographic Creative; **40–41** ©Ociacia/Shutterstock.com; **42–43** ©Shawn Rocco/Duke Medicine; **44** (t) Mike Chorost; **45** (t) Randy Quan/Toronto Star/Getty Images; **46** (t) Camera Press/Jane Barlow/Redux Pictures; **48** (b) Shawn Poynter/The New York Times/Redux Pictures; **50–51** ©James Duncan Davidson/TED; **53** (c) Pedro Henrique Ferreira/TED; **54** (c) Pedro Henrique Ferreira/TED; **55** (t) Emotiv Inc/National Geographic Creative; **56–57** Earth Welty/Aurora Photos; **58–59** AF archive/Alamy; **60** Adapted from Diener and Scollon (2003) Retrieved from: http://www.lidata.eu/index.php?file=files/eng/training/en_seminar_201012/semin_201012.html&course_file=semin_201012_2.html; **61** (t) China Stringer Network/Reuters; **62** (b) Miguel Costa; **66–67** James Duncan Davidson/TED; **68** (bl) Adapted from Marks, N. (2013, 9th October) The Happy Planet Index [webpage]. Retrieved from http://www.happinessworks.com/blog/2013/10/09/the-happy-planet-index/; **71** (t) Diane Cook/Len Jenshel/National Geographic Creative; **72–73** Carl David Granback/National Geographic Creative; **74–75** ©Winston Chen; **76** (t) ©Winston Chen; **80** (b) Matthew Stewart Bennett/Moment Select/Getty Images; **82–83** ©Marla Aufmuth/TED; **86** (b) Joost van den Broek/Hollandse Hoogte/Redux Pictures; **87** (t) AP Images/Joseph Kaczmarek; **88–89** Aaron Huey/National Geographic Creative; **90–91** (t) Brian Yen; **93** (c) ©Lab 42; **97** (b) Elizabeth Stevens/National Geographic; **98–99** ©James Duncan Davidson/TED; **103** (t) The Washington Post/Getty Images; **104–105** Mahmoud Zayyat/AFP/Getty Images; **106–107** Mario Tama/Getty Images; **108** (cr) ©Nicemonkey/Shutterstock.com; **108** (cl) ©360b/Shutterstock.com; **108** (cr) ©Pockygallery/Shutterstock.com; **108** (bl) (bc) ©Filip Bjorkman/Shutterstock.com; **108** (bc) ©Robert Biedermann/Shutterstock.com; **108** (bc) ©Stefanina Hill/Shutterstock.com; **108** (bc) ©Volina/Shutterstock.com; **109** (t) Panos Pictures; **113** (b) ©Aziz Abu Sarah; **114–115** (t) ©James Duncan Davidson/TED; **118** (bl) Monterey Media/Everett Collection; **119** (t) Peter Mountain/Walt Disney Pictures/Everett Collection; **120–121** Krista Rossow/National Geographic Creative; **122–123** David Trood/The Image Bank/Getty Images; **124** (br) Lisa Peardon/The Image Bank/Getty Images; **125** (t) Tony Avelar/Bloomberg/Getty Images; **127** (tl) Jamie Garbutt/The Image Bank/Getty Images; **127** (tr) Yuri_Arcurs/E+/Getty Images; **127** (cl) David Freund/Photodisc/Getty Images; **127** (cr) Wonwoo Lee/Image Source/Getty Images; **130–131** ©James Duncan Davidson/TED; **133** (b) Michael S Yamashita/Encyclopedia/Corbis; **135** (t) Margaret Bourke-White/Time & Life Pictures/Getty Images; **136–137** Cyril Ruoso/Minden Pictures; **138–139** Jeff Rotman/Minden Pictures; **140** (t) William Albert Allard/National Geographic Image Collection; **141** (b) Auscape/UIG/Getty Images; **143** (b) Hugo Van Lawick/National Geographic Creative; **146–147** Frans Lanting/National Geographic Creative; **151** (t) Jurgen Freund/Minden Pictures; **152–153** Joey Schuster; **154–155** (t) Pictorial Press Ltd/Alamy; **156** (br) Kimberly Hosey/Moment/Getty Images; **157** (b) Source: helpguide.org; **161** (b) AFP/Getty Images; **163** ©James Duncan Davidson/TED; **165** (b) NASA digital version copyright/Latitude/Corbis; **167** (t) Tiffany Brown/Redux; **176** ©James Duncan Davidson/TED; **177** (br) Medford Taylor/National Geographic Creative; **178–179** Michael Brands/TED; **180** ©James Duncan Davidson/TED; **181** (b) Pedro Henrique Ferreira/TED; **182** ©James Duncan Davidson/TED; **183** (b) ©Miguel Costa; **184** ©Marla Aufmuth/TED; **185** (b) Joost van den Broek/Hollandse Hoogte/Redux Pictures; **186** ©James Duncan Davidson/TED; **187** (b) Brian Yen; **188–189** (b) ©James Duncan Davidson/TED; **190** ©James Duncan Davidson/TED; **191** (b) Lisa Peardon/The Image Bank/Getty Images; **192–193** (b) Franz Lanting/National Geographic Creative; **194** ©James Duncan Davidson/TED; **195** (b) NASA digital version copyright/Latitude/Corbis.